Blocks and Chains
Introduction to Bitcoin, Cryptocurrencies,
and Their Consensus Mechanisms

Synthesis Lectures on Information Security, Privacy, & Trust

Editors

Elisa Bertino, *Purdue University*
Ravi Sandhu, *University of Texas, San Antonio*

The Synthesis Lectures Series on Information Security, Privacy, and Trust publishes 50- to 100-page publications on topics pertaining to all aspects of the theory and practice of Information Security, Privacy, and Trust. The scope largely follows the purview of premier computer security research journals such as ACM Transactions on Information and System Security, IEEE Transactions on Dependable and Secure Computing and Journal of Cryptology, and premier research conferences, such as ACM CCS, ACM SACMAT, ACM AsiaCCS, ACM CODASPY, IEEE Security and Privacy, IEEE Computer Security Foundations, ACSAC, ESORICS, Crypto, EuroCrypt and AsiaCrypt. In addition to the research topics typically covered in such journals and conferences, the series also solicits lectures on legal, policy, social, business, and economic issues addressed to a technical audience of scientists and engineers. Lectures on significant industry developments by leading practitioners are also solicited.

Blocks and Chains: Introduction to Bitcoin, Cryptocurrencies, and Their Consensus Mechanisms
Aljosha Judmayer, Nicholas Stifter, Katharina Krombholz, and Edgar Weippl

ISBN: 978-3-031-01224-2 paperback
ISBN: 978-3-031-02352-1 ebook

DOI 10.1007/978-3-031-02352-1

A Publication in the Springer series
SYNTHESIS LECTURES ON INFORMATION SECURITY, PRIVACY, & TRUST

Lecture #20
Series Editors: Elisa Bertino, *Purdue University*
                Ravi Sandhu, *University of Texas, San Antonio*
Series ISSN
Print 1945-9742   Electronic 1945-9750

Blocks and Chains

Introduction to Bitcoin, Cryptocurrencies, and Their Consensus Mechanisms

Aljosha Judmayer, Nicholas Stifter, Katharina Krombholz, and Edgar Weippl
SBA Research

SYNTHESIS LECTURES ON INFORMATION SECURITY, PRIVACY, & TRUST #20

ABSTRACT

The new field of cryptographic currencies and consensus ledgers, commonly referred to as *blockchains*, is receiving increasing interest from various different communities. These communities are very diverse and amongst others include: technical enthusiasts, activist groups, researchers from various disciplines, start-ups, large enterprises, public authorities, banks, financial regulators, business men, investors, and also criminals. The scientific community adapted relatively slowly to this emerging and fast-moving field of cryptographic currencies and consensus ledgers. This was one reason that, for quite a while, the only resources available have been the Bitcoin source code, blog and forum posts, mailing lists, and other online publications. Also the original Bitcoin paper which initiated the hype was published online without any prior peer review. Following the original publication spirit of the Bitcoin paper, a lot of innovation in this field has repeatedly come from the community itself in the form of online publications and online conversations instead of established peer-reviewed scientific publishing. On the one side, this spirit of fast free software development, combined with the business aspects of cryptographic currencies, as well as the interests of today's time-to-market focused industry, produced a flood of publications, whitepapers, and prototypes. On the other side, this has led to deficits in systematization and a gap between practice and the theoretical understanding of this new field. This book aims to further close this gap and presents a well-structured overview of this broad field from a technical viewpoint. The archetype for modern cryptographic currencies and consensus ledgers is Bitcoin and its underlying Nakamoto consensus. Therefore we describe the inner workings of this protocol in great detail and discuss its relations to other derived systems.

KEYWORDS

block, chain, blockchain, Bitcoin, cryptographic currency, Proof-of-Work, Nakamoto consensus, consensus ledger

Contents

Acknowledgments

This research was funded by COMET K1, FFG–Austrian Research Promotion Agency, FFG Bridge Early Stage 846573 A2Bit and FFG Bridge 1 858561 SESC. We want to thank our reviewers, Foteini Baldimtsi, Patrick McCorry and Jong Ho Won, for useful feedback and discussions.

Aljosha Judmayer, Nicholas Stifter, Katharina Krombholz, and Edgar Weippl
May 2017

CHAPTER 1

Introduction

Since the introduction of Bitcoin [117] as a prototype for a decentralized cryptocurrency between 2008 and 2009, the field of cryptocurrency technologies has experienced a rapid growth in popularity. Those technologies that are based on the same or very similar fundamental principles as Bitcoin are commonly referred to as *blockchains*. The term *blockchain* itself was not directly introduced by Satoshi Nakamoto in the original paper [117], but used early on within the Bitcoin community to refer to certain concepts of the cryptocurrency. As a result, there are two common spellings of this term found throughout the literature, namely *blockchain* and *block chain*. Although, the later variant was used by Satoshi Nakamoto in a comment within the original source code,[1] the first one is used frequently in press articles as well as recent academic literature e.g., in publications such as [50], and has established itself as the de facto standard. Therefore, we will use the term *blockchain* throughout this book. Nowadays *blockchain* is used as a nebulous umbrella term to refer to various concepts that are related to cryptocurrency technologies. One goal of this book is to demystify this term and provide a solid introduction to the field it encompasses, i.e., distributed cryptocurrencies, their underlying technologies, as well as their governing consensus mechanisms.

To date, over 700 different cryptocurrencies have been created [1]. Some of those currencies only had a very short lifespan or were merely conceived for fraudulent purposes, while others brought additional innovations and still have vital and vibrant communities today.

The mechanisms and underlying principles of most of these cryptocurrencies are, to a greater or lesser extent, derived from the original Bitcoin protocol. Several of these incarnations may only differ from Bitcoin in their choice of certain constants such as the target block interval or maximum number of currency units that will eventually come into existence. Others have switched to alternative proof-of-work algorithms (e.g., Litecoin [129], Dogecoin [128]), have included additional features (e.g., Namecoin [2], Ethereum [66], Zcash [64]), or have used different distributed consensus approaches (e.g., PeerCoin [96], Ripple [133]).

In the few years since the launch of Bitcoin, the decentralized cryptocurrency has grown to remarkable economic value and currently has a market capitalization of around 17 billion USD.[2]

---

[1] https://github.com/trottier/original-bitcoin/blob/master/src/main.h#L795-L803
[2] This marked rise in valuation, but also the high volatility of the currency, has made it difficult to provide an estimate that is not quickly superseded and appears hopelessly outdated.

This has not only led to extensive news coverage but also to an increased interest from different communities reaching from technical enthusiasts to business people and investors to criminals and law enforcement agencies.

Mainstream media coverage of security incidents and popular myths around Bitcoin show that its fundamentals are hard to understand for non-expert users and cannot be reconciled with the mental models of traditional currency systems.

Bitcoin was designed to be a decentralized cryptographic currency that does not rely on trusted third parties. It achieves this by combining clever incentive engineering and the right cryptographic primitives with a novel probabilistic distributed consensus approach. This combination and the practical demonstration of its feasibility are proving to be a significant contribution that has the potential to profoundly impact other domains beyond cryptocurrencies. These implications are increasingly gaining attention from the scientific community and relate to other security problems of distributed systems, such as distributed name spaces, secure timestamping, and many more.

All these circumstances make the deployment of Bitcoin as a financial instrument an exciting experiment for researchers in many fields. As stated by Bonneau et al. [27], *"Bitcoin is a rare case where practice seems to be ahead of theory. We consider that a tremendous opportunity for the research community to tackle the many open questions about Bitcoin …."*

Hence, the use of the underlying technologies, commonly referred to as *blockchain*, has been progressively covered in scientific literature and is more and more finding its way to consumer applications. Despite the rising interest within academia as well as the private sector, many open problems remain in terms of finding a balance between performance, scalability, security, decentralization, and anonymity in such systems.

1.1   ASPECTS OF CRYPTOCURRENCIES

Cryptocurrencies have many different aspects, and can therefore be viewed from various angles, including the *financial and economic perspective*, *legal perspective*, *political and sociological perspective*, as well as *technical* and *socio-technical perspectives*. These very different viewpoints can be separated even further; for example, the technical aspects can be divided into the following non-exhaustive list of fields: *cryptography*, *network and distributed systems*, *game theory*, *data science*, and *software and language security*. In this book, the focus is placed on the **technical perspectives** that are necessary to understand this broad field. In doing so, we also discuss aspects of *human-computer interaction* and *usable security*, which are vital for the adoption of a cryptographic currency and, therefore, also related to the overall level of security a cryptographic currency can offer.

1.2   CRYPTOCURRENCY COMMUNITY

The cryptographic currency community is as diverse as the possible viewpoints on the topic. Cryptocurrencies are, as the name suggests, intended to be used as currencies. Therefore, they attract a variety of different people, including *technology enthusiasts, businesses and investors, ideologists, researchers, cypherpunks, libertarians, public authorities and policy makers, financial regulators, banks*, and also *criminals*, who exploit anonymity measures and make use of the fact that criminal investigation and de-anonymization techniques are lagging behind. In contrast to that, the distributed nature of Bitcoin-like cryptocurrencies also attracts activists and individuals living in oppressive regimes, as these enable them to manage their digital assets despite political sanctions. This highlights the important role that decentralized currencies can play for inhabitants of such countries.

This composition of the broader Bitcoin community as well as its loose structure, combined with a strong mindset of avoiding trusted single points of failure, might also be one reason why it is sometimes hard to reach consensus regarding the direction of Bitcoin's technological development, as interests might diverge. This book aims to not engage in currently ongoing debates (e.g., regarding the maximum block size) but rather to present a neutral, fact-based introduction to this broad topic.

Following the traditional publication spirit of Satoshi Nakamoto, many papers in this field are self-published or made available online as pre-prints prior to their acceptance at scientific journals or conferences. Therefore, we opted to also reference online resources and pre-prints that have not yet been published in peer reviewed venues. The authors are furthermore maintaining a public bibliography[3] where all references that are made in this book can be found.

1.3   FROM CRYPTOCURRENCY TO BLOCKCHAIN

Early works in the area of cryptographic currencies or *cryptocurrencies* mostly focused on required cryptographic primitives as well as the privacy guarantees that could be achieved in such systems [41, 42, 43]. Thereby, these systems themselves still had to rely on trusted third parties (TTPs) to be able to guarantee correct operation. This necessity changed in 2009 when Bitcoin was launched as the first *decentralized* distributed currency [117] that removed the dependency on TTPs. Bitcoin achieves this through a novel combination of well known primitives and techniques, such as, for example, proof-of-work (PoW), to eventually establish agreement (or *consensus*) amongst all nodes on the state of the underlying transaction ledger. The resulting consensus approach, termed *Nakamoto consensus* [27], allows for permissionless participation [147] by potentially *anonymous* actors.

One core element of Bitcoin and Nakamoto consensus is the *blockchain*. Originally the term *blockchain* was used to refer to the aggregation and agreement on transactions in an immutable ledger. Now *blockchain* is used as an umbrella term to refer to all kinds of cryptocurrency

---

[3]Bibliography: https://allquantor.at/blockchainbib.

technologies. This set of technologies and techniques is also commonly referred to as *blockchain technologies* [32]. Although the term *blockchain* is often not well defined, a rough distinction can be made between *permissionless blockchains*, where participation in the consensus algorithm, at least in principle, is not restricted, and *permissioned blockchain*, where there is a closed set of nodes amongst which consensus has to be reached. For a more detailed definition of the term *blockchain* as used in this book see Section 4.2.2.

1.4   THE ANALOG STONE-BLOCK-CHAIN

Capturing and effectively conveying the basic principles of Bitcoin and other blockchain-based cryptocurrencies to novices, especially those without a technical background, can be a difficult task. When trying to explain the technological innovation and novel approach presented by Bitcoin, you are quickly faced with the problem of having to refer to complex elements such as consensus algorithms and cryptography.

This section provides a completely *analog* example that may be helpful when trying to explain the fundamental mechanisms of blockchain technologies to people without the necessary technological background knowledge. The example of the *stone-block-chain* replaces Bitcoin's complex components with simple, real-world analogies, and while it is, of course, not able to accurately cover all the details, it should capture the basic ideas. Practicality aside, the described system should help illustrate the basic principles of blockchain-based cryptocurrencies.

Nakamotopia: In a land far away, there is a stone age village called *Nakamotopia* whose inhabitants are famous for their stone carvers and general obsession with stone blocks. Up until recently, the Nakamotopians relied on small, round, intricately carved rocks as their currency and medium of exchange. However, crafty individuals found a process that allowed them to easily and quickly carve new rocks and subsequently both the value and trust in the currency was quickly lost in the wake of hyperinflation. In dire need of a new currency, the village elders called for an emergency meeting to discuss the future of the Nakamotopian financial system. Their solution was an ingenious idea for a stone-block-chain that combines the Nakamotopians' obsession with stone blocks and their attraction toward lottery systems. The following three-step scheme was devised, which the Nakamotopians called the block creation ceremony:

Miner selection: Every day, all Nakamotopians meet in the village square. In the first part of the block creation ceremony, every villager puts one small stone, engraved with their (unique) name, into a big wooden box. Thereby, the other villagers oversee the process and check that every villager acts honestly.

This box is then placed on a geyser next to the village. During the selection ceremony, all villagers wait for the geyser to erupt and eject steam so that the box containing all the stones is propelled high up into the air and scatters its contents. The villager whose stone lands closest to the geyser wins the lottery and is elected as the *miner* of the next block.

Figure 1.1: Nakamotopian random miner selection by geyser.

Transaction processing: After a villager has been selected as miner for that day, she has the duty to collect all transactions from the villagers that have not yet been recorded. The villagers who want to perform transactions queue up in front of the miner to inform her about transactions that should be included in the stone-block-chain. A transaction transfers ownership of a certain number of currency units from one name to another and is only valid if the sender actually has at least as many units as he wants to transfer to the receiver. The only exception to this rule is the first transaction that is engraved into the block, which credits the miner with a predetermined number of units as a reward for her efforts. This special miner transaction is also the only way in which new currency units can be created. At the end of this session, the stone block will contain all the transactions the miner has decided to include. The remaining space of the stone block will be filled with the holy termination symbol 0x00 so that no additional transactions can be added, i.e., engraved, later on without being detected. If someone were to polish the entire surface of the stone block to engrave a completely new set of transactions, this would be detectable, since all blocks must have exactly the same dimensions. During this whole process, the chosen miner is allowed to not include a particular transaction. If this happens, the person who wants the transaction to be included into a stone block has to wait until the next day and hope that the next miner will include the transaction.

Figure 1.2: Transaction processing by engraving transactions into empty stone blocks.

Chaining: After the miner has prepared the current stone block, it is heaved toward the town center. Because of the tremendous size and weight of such a stone block, it takes the combined effort of a large number of villagers to move it at all. If a miner were to engrave invalid transactions or otherwise create a stone block that does not obey the rules that were set out by the elders, no honest villager would help the miner move the block. This ensures that the miner sticks to the rules and does not forfeit her chance to receive the mining reward.

Once a valid stone block has been moved by the villagers into the town center, they lift it on top of the towering stack of previous blocks. Only once a block is placed onto this stack is it considered valid by the Nakamotopians.

Stacking the stone blocks has several advantages: Not only does it establish a logical order of transactions, it also makes it much more difficult to change blocks that are further down in the past. An attacker would need to persuade a large number of villagers to start taking off blocks from the top, each requiring a significant amount of time and effort to be removed, which would not remain unnoticed by honest villagers for very long. On the other hand, if a large number of villagers come to the conclusion that one or several blocks should not belong on top of the chain, they can collectively remove these blocks and replace them, thereby ensuring that the majority always agrees upon the contents of their stone-block-chain.

1.4.1 SECURITY MODEL OF THE STONE-BLOCK-CHAIN

We will now look at the security guarantees such a stone-block-chain can offer and how this analogy relates to the properties current cryptographic currency technologies aim to provide.

Public transaction ledger As with Bitcoin, all transactions that take place in Nakamotopia are recorded in a publicly accessible chain of blocks. The key difference here is that Bitcoin is a pseudonymous system, whereas the Nakamotopians use their real identities in their transactions.

Proof-of-Work The basic requirement for a proof-of-work (PoW) should be that it is hard to produce but easy to verify. In Bitcoin, the PoW also functions as a leader election mechanism that randomly selects a new leader, i.e., creator of a valid PoW, on every new block.

In the stone-block-chain analogy, the properties of the proof-of-work are split into three parts. (I) The work that has been put into crafting the blank blocks beforehand and placing the current one at the top of the chain on town square aims to fulfill the "hard to produce" criterion. (II) Once a block has been placed onto the stone-block-chain, it is still easy to verify by reading the transactions engraved onto it and measuring its dimensions to verify that it complies with the rules defining a valid block layout. (III) The geyser in our example works as a random leader-election mechanism on every new stone-block. In Bitcoin, this is achieved through the probabilistic properties of computing a valid PoW for blocks.

Immutability Since every stone block is huge and has precisely defined dimensions, it is unlikely that the effort required for changing a previous stone block in the chain will go unnoticed by several honest Nakamotopians. Even if someone manages to craft a completely new stone block that includes malicious transactions, the effort of replacing an older block in the chain will be detected by some villagers living next to the town square and would also require the collaboration of many dishonest Nakamotopians to be feasible.

In Bitcoin, the blocks are chained together by cryptographic hash functions.

Honest majority   Assuming that the majority of villagers are honest, a large portion of the stacked chain of blocks comes from honest villagers and will eventually cease to be in danger of being changed by malicious villagers. Initially there is a slight chance that some of the topmost blocks that have been added to the chain came from malicious villagers while the larger portion of honest Nakamotopians were occupied with other, more pressing issues. Once they return, this honest majority can set about removing the invalid blocks and start replacing them. On the other hand, it takes time for the minority of dishonest villagers to remove or add blocks and both can be quickly detected by any honest villager. If there are enough new stone blocks stacked upon a particular block, it would take the dishonest villagers many days to remove them, making such an attack very unlikely to succeed. Therefore, stone blocks that have been included far enough in the past (i.e., lower in the chain) can be considered agreed upon.

Bitcoin blocks that have a high number of confirmations, i.e., blocks appended after them, are unlikely to change and can, therefore, be considered agreed upon. Although the number of confirmation blocks depends on the value of the transaction in question, common wisdom is that six confirmation blocks are enough to consider a past transaction secure [69].

1.5   STRUCTURE OF THIS BOOK

The remainder of this book is structured as follows: Following a brief introduction of notations and definitions in Chapter 2, Chapter 3 provides a brief overview of the history of cryptocurrencies that led to the invention of Bitcoin. Chapter 4 discusses Bitcoin as the archetype of modern distributed proof-of-work-based cryptocurrencies and highlights the basic properties of blockchain and distributed ledger technologies. Chapter 5 provides an overview of human interactions with cryptocurrency ecosystems on the example of Bitcoin. This highlights the challenges in the area of digital assets management and presents a discussion of Bitcoin usability, privacy, and security challenges from the user's perspective. Chapter 6 addresses the Nakamoto consensus in the context of distributed fault-tolerant computing and highlights the developments toward modeling this new consensus approach. Chapter 7, finally, provides an outlook on future developments of cryptocurrencies and other applications of blockchain technology. For further studies we point the reader to our public bibliography[4] that holds additional references that go beyond the scope of this book.

---

[4]Bibliography: https://allquantor.at/blockchainbib.

CHAPTER 2

Background

This chapter provides a high-level overview of the cryptographic primitives required in the domain of cryptocurrency technologies, as well as explanations of the symbols and notations that are used throughout the book. For the background on distributed fault tolerant computing see Chapter 6.

2.1 CRYPTOGRAPHIC PRIMITIVES

In this section we outline the cryptographic primitives that are required to understand the principles of current PoW-based cryptocurrencies. On a high level the two basic buildings blocks in this context are *cryptographic hash functions* and *asymmetric cryptography*.

2.1.1 CRYPTOGRAPHIC HASH FUNCTIONS

The most important primitive in the context of PoW-based cryptocurrencies are *cryptographic hash functions*. Therefore, we focus on the properties required from such functions as well as the constructions that can be based on it, e.g., *Merkle trees*. While describing the basic properties, we will not go into much detail regarding the security guaranties of the discussed schemes.

Hash function: A hash function H takes a message x of arbitrary but finite size and outputs a fixed size hash h (also called digest). When not explicitly stated differently, we refer to a *cryptographic hash function* whenever the term *hash function* is used in this book.

Cryptographic hash function: There are four additional properties of a hash function that have to be fulfilled so that the function qualifies as a *cryptographic* hash function [106].

1. **Easy to compute:** It is computationally easy to calculate the hash of any given finite message.

$$h = H(x), \text{ Where } h \text{ is of fixed length.} \tag{2.1}$$

2. **Pre-image resistance:** It is infeasible to generate a message that has a given hash value. Infeasible in this context means it cannot be achieved by an adversary as long as the security of the message is important. In terms of complexity theory, this is defined as not being possible in polynomial time. Because of this property, cryptographic hash functions are also called one-way functions.

$$\text{Given a hash } h \text{ it is infeasible to find any message } x \text{ such that } h = H(x). \tag{2.2}$$

3. **Second pre-image resistance:** It is infeasible to find two different messages which produce identical outputs, i.e., a collision, when given as input to the hash function.

$$\text{Given a message } m \text{ it is infeasible to find another message } m' \\ \text{such that } m \neq m' \text{ and } H(m) = H(m'). \tag{2.3}$$

4. **Collision resistance:** It is infeasible to find *any* two different messages which produce identical outputs, i.e., a collision, when given as input to the hash function.

$$\text{It is infeasible to find any two messages } m, m' \\ \text{where } m \neq m' \text{ and } H(m) = H(m'). \tag{2.4}$$

Merkle tree: In the paper [107] Merkle introduced the concept of a one-time signature scheme that relies on a *"infinite tree of one-time signatures."* This underlying concept later became known as a *Merkle tree, hash tree*, or *authentication tree* [106]. Merkle trees are binary trees in which the leaf nodes are labeled with the values that need to be authenticated and each non-leaf node is labeled with the hash of the labels or values of its child nodes. Figure 2.1 shows an example Merkle tree with $n = 4$ values and the resulting *root hash* or Merkle tree root r. To authenticate a value v_1 and prove that it was part of a Merkle tree with root hash r, the values h_2 and h_6 are required. For more information on Merkle trees see [14].

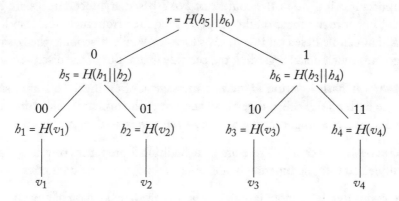

Figure 2.1: Example Merkle tree with $n = 4$ values. Nodes are referenced with a binary string representing their position, e.g., node 01 is labeled h_2.

Some properties of such a tree structure are:

- The length of the path from any leaf to the root of a (balanced) binary tree with n leafs is approximated by $log_2(n)$.

- Given a root hash r and a value v, it requires approximately $log_2(n)$ hash computations to prove that v is indeed a leaf of a (balanced) binary tree.

2.1.2 ASYMMETRIC CRYPTOGRAPHY

The second most important primitive on which cryptographic currencies are based is *asymmetric cryptography*. Since cryptographic currency technologies mostly rely on well researched algorithms and parameters in this context (e.g., Bitcoin uses Secp256k1 [38]), we will not go into detail regarding the aspects concerning this broad field of research.

For further details as well as the mathematical foundations of the topics mentioned in this section please refer to [6, 26, 28, 46, 86, 89, 91].

Public-key encryption: A *public-key encryption* scheme is defined as a triple of efficient algorithms $\mathscr{E} = (G, E, D)$ where,

- G is a key generation algorithm that takes no input and outputs a key pair (pk, sk), where pk is called public key, which can be shared publicly, and sk is called secret key, which should be kept private.

$$(pk, sk) \leftarrow G(). \qquad (2.5)$$

- E is a encryption algorithm that takes as input a public-key pk as well as a message $m \in \mathcal{M}$ and outputs a cipher text $c \in C$ encrypted under the public-key pk associated with the public/secret key pair (pk, sk) of the intended recipient.

$$c \leftarrow E(pk, m). \qquad (2.6)$$

- D is a (deterministic) decryption algorithm that takes as input a secret-key sk as well as a cipher text $c \in C$ and outputs the message $m \in \mathcal{M}$, that was encrypted under the public-key pk associated with sk, or $\perp$ if the wrong keys have been used.

$$m \leftarrow D(sk, c). \qquad (2.7)$$

It follows that if the respective operations are reversible $\forall (pk, sk)$ of G it holds that:

$$\forall m \in \mathcal{M} : D(sk, E(pk, m)) = m. \qquad (2.8)$$

Digital signatures: A *digital signature* scheme is defined as a triple of efficient algorithms $\mathscr{S} = (G, S, V)$ where,

- G is a key generation algorithm that takes no input and outputs a key pair (pk, sk), where pk is called public key, which can be shared publicly, and sk is called secret key, which should be kept private.

$$(pk, sk) \leftarrow G(). \qquad (2.9)$$

- S is a signing algorithm that takes as input a secret key sk as well as a message $m \in \mathcal{M}$ and outputs a signature $\sigma \in \Sigma$ that can be communicated publicly together with the message. S is invoked as

$$S : \sigma \leftarrow E(sk, m). \qquad (2.10)$$

- V is a (deterministic) algorithm that takes as input a public-key pk a message $m \in \mathcal{M}$ as well as a signature $\sigma \in \Sigma$ and outputs either `accept` or `reject` depending on the validity of the signature σ on message m.

$$\{\text{accept}, \text{reject}\} \leftarrow V(pk, m, \sigma). \tag{2.11}$$

If follows that a signature generated by S is accepted by V iff (pk, sk) is a valid public/secret key pair. So $\forall (pk, sk)$ of G it holds that:

$$\forall m \in \mathcal{M} : V(pk, m, S(sk, m)) = \text{accept}. \tag{2.12}$$

2.2   NOTATION, SYMBOLS, AND DEFINITIONS

This section provides an overview of the notations and symbols used throughout the book (Table 2.1).

Table 2.1: Notations, symbols, and definitions used in this book

Symbols	Description	Sections
$0xff$	The prefix 0x denotes a hexadecimal representation. In this case the hexadecimal representation of the decimal number 255.	4
$\|\|$	String concatination.	-
$x[251:255]$	Refers to the bits from 251 to 255 of variable x.	-
$H()$	Cryptographically secure hash function.	2.1; 4.3
$H^x()$	Chained use of function x times e.g., $H^2(i) = H(H(i))$.	-
$SHA\ 256()$	The cryptographic hash function SHA256 as defined in [119].	-
T	The target defines the validity and hardness of a proof-of-work. In Bitcoin a valid PoW is defined as: $$SHA256^2(\text{block header}) \leq T.$$	4
z	Number of leading *zero bits* of the 256 bit number T.	4
$Pr(x)$	Probability of x, $0 \leq Pr(x) \leq 1$.	-
$m(p)$	Number of attempts a process p can make when searching for a PoW solution in a unit of time.	-
Π	Set of processes $\{p_1, p_2, ..., p_n\} = \Pi$.	-
$\mathcal{B}(t)$	Subset of Byzantine nodes $\mathcal{B} \subseteq \Pi$ at time t.	-
f	Number of faulty processes, $0 \leq f \leq n$ where n denotes the total number of processes.	-
$\Diamond\mathcal{W}, \mathcal{P},$ $\Diamond\mathcal{S}(bz), \Diamond\mathcal{M}_{\mathcal{A}}$	Different classes of Failure Detectors.	6.2.2

CHAPTER 3

History of Cryptographic Currencies

The history of cryptographic currencies rests on two foundations. The first is the history of distributed systems research in general, and the second is the history of electronic cash systems. In the early days, these two areas of research had very few connections with each other, despite the use of cryptographic primitives. Both fields are related to research and advances in cryptography, and particularly research in the area of electronic cash was driven by the inventions in the area of asymmetric cryptography, e.g., blind signature schemes. In retrospect, Bitcoin provided the missing link between those fields of research to create a *decentralized* cryptographic currency. Bitcoin cherry-picked the right pieces from each of these areas and combined them. One byproduct of the rise of Bitcoin is an increased interest in distributed systems research as well as in electronic payment systems and currencies.

In this chapter, we take a brief look at the history of cryptographic currencies before Bitcoin and the beginnings of this field of research. Therefore we focus on the technical innovations and the context of existing research at that time rather than individual persons or legal definitions. The purpose of this chapter is to provide a basic understanding of historical events that impacted cryptocurrency research and the community around it.

Legally cryptographic currencies of all types fall under the definition of a virtual currency. The term *virtual currency* was defined by the European Central Bank in 2014 as "a digital representation of value that is neither issued by a central bank or a public authority, nor necessarily attached to a fiat currency, but is accepted by natural or legal persons as a means of payment and can be transferred, stored or traded electronically" [9].

In Chapter 6, we describe the history from a distributed systems perspective.

3.1 BEFORE BITCOIN

This section covers the roots as well as the early days of cryptographic currency research, from the original idea and steadily improving concepts and implementations until the point that Bitcoin was born.

3.1.1   THE EARLY BEGINNINGS OF DIGITAL CASH

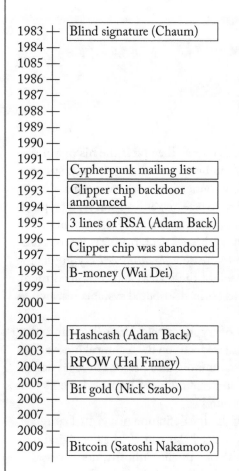

The history of cryptographic currencies started in the 1980s with David Chaum's work [42, 43]. He is commonly referred to as the inventor of secure digital cash for his paper on cryptographic primitives of blind signatures [41]. In this paper, Chaum proposed a novel cryptographic scheme to blind the content of a message before it is signed, so that the signer cannot determine the content. These *blind signatures* can be publicly verified just like a regular digital signature. Chaum's proposed digital cash approach allows users to spend a digital currency in such a way that it is untraceable by another party. In a later publication, Chaum et al. [43] improved the idea by allowing offline transactions and by adding double-spending detection mechanisms. Nevertheless, the system requires trusted parties for issuing and clearance of electronic cash.

To commercialize his ideas of digital cash, Chaum founded DigiCash in 1990. This *first generation* of cryptographic currencies failed to reach a broad audience despite various commercialization efforts [3].

3.1.2   THE CYPHERPUNK MOVEMENT

With David Chaum's advances in the field, the cypherpunk movement was born. The informal group communicated via the Cypherpunks electronic mailing list and advocated the use of cryptography and privacy-enhancing technologies. Among others, David Chaum's work inspired the group of activists to promote the widespread use of these technologies. Before that, cryptography was not publicly available to consumers and exclusively practiced by the military and intelligence agencies. The Cypherpunk movement addressed topics such as anonymity, pseudonymity, communication privacy and data hiding, but also censorship and monitoring. A major issue in the mid-1990s was the Clipper chip chipset developed by the NSA, which was heavily criticized by the Cypherpunks for its built-in backdoor. In 1994, Matt Blaze published a paper on vulnerabilities in Clipper Chip's escrow system [25]. He found that the chip transmitted information that could be exploited to recover the encryption key in a specific *Law Enforcement Access Field (LEAF)*. This LEAF contained a 16 bit hash to prove that the message has not been modified. 16 bit however were not sufficient as a reliable integrity measure, as an attacker could easily brute force another

LEAF value that would give the same hash but not the correct keys after an attempted escrow. Further vulnerabilities were detected in 1995 by Moti Yung and Yair Frankel who in their work showed that key escrow device tracking can further be exploited by attaching the LEAF to messages from different devices than the originating one to bypass escrow in real time [74]. Several other attacks have been published since then, e.g., [4], and activist groups, such as the Electronic Frontier Foundation, also expressed their concerns about the Clipper chip and the government's efforts to limit the use of encryption by Internet users. This is commonly referred to as crypto wars. The inventor of Hashcash, Adam Back, pioneered the use of ultra-compact code with his 3-line RSA in Perl signature file which was then printed on t-shirts to protest the United States' cryptography export regulations. Due to the lack of adoption of the Clipper chip by smartphone manufacturers, the design was abandoned in 1996. However, the debate on key escrow and government-controlled backdoors persists even to this date. The Snowden revelations of 2013 sparked a public wave of concern that resulted in an increased demand for cryptographic applications by end users and vendors.

3.1.3   THE RISE OF CRYPTOCURRENCIES

Before the first decentralized cryptocurrency, Bitcoin, and its successors emerged, a number of approaches that improved on the original idea of David Chaum were proposed. These concepts represent incremental improvements, but as they still contained centralized elements, they do not qualify as completely decentralized currencies.

b-money: In 1998, Wei Dai proposed b-money [53], an anonymous and distributed electronic cash system. In his proposal, he described two protocols based on the assumption that an untraceable network exists where senders and receivers are identified only by digital pseudonyms such as their public keys, and that every message is signed by its sender and encrypted to the receiver. B-money also allowed the creation of money based on previously unsolved cryptographic puzzles.

bit gold: In 1998, Nick Szabo designed a new digital currency called *bit gold*. His system also relied on cryptographic puzzles which, after being solved, were sent to a Byzantine fault-tolerant public registry and assigned to the public key of the solver. This allowed network consensus over new coins to be obtained. To address the problem of double-spending without a central authority, Szabo's scheme was designed to mimic the trust characteristics of gold. In 2002, Szabo also presented a theory of collectibles based on the origins of money [144].

Hashcash: Adam Back proposed Hashcash [10], a proof-of-work (PoW) system based on cryptographic hash functions to derive probabilistic proof of computational work as an authentication mechanism. The requirements of this system were that, on the one hand, it should be hard to find a valid solution, but on the other, it should be easy to verify any given solution. With Hashcash, the purpose of the PoW was to ensure that it was computationally hard for a spammer to transmit mails over an anonymous mail relay [10]. Since the identity of the sender should be protected, no traditional authentication checks are possible in such a scenario. Therefore, the mail server required the solution to a computational challenge as an authentication method for accepting the message for relaying. In the case of Hashcash, this was realized via an additional e-mail header. Back's PoW scheme was conceptually reused in Bitcoin mining.

RPOW: Based on previous work, Hal Finney presented the first currency system based on a reusable proof-of-work (RPOW) and Szabo's theory of collectibles [144] in 2004 [70]. Similar to Szabo's bit gold, Finney's scheme introduced token money that was aligned with the concept of gold value. Later, after the launch of Bitcoin, Hal Finney became the first user of this new distributed cryptocurrency after Satoshi Nakamoto. He received a Bitcoin transaction from Bitcoin's creator Satoshi Nakamoto.

3.2   BITCOIN

Between 2008 and 2009, Bitcoin was created as the first decentralized cryptocurrency by the pseudonymous developer Satoshi Nakamoto [117]. Nakamoto self-published the Bitcoin whitepaper in 2008 and soon after, on January 3rd, 2009, the genesis block of the Bitcoin protocol was created, marking the start of Bitcoin as a decentralized cryptocurrency. To date, it is by far the most successful cryptocurrency in terms of market capitalization. More than 700 altcoins (e.g., Litecoin, Peercoin) based on Bitcoin have been proposed since the launch of Bitcoin.

C H A P T E R   4

Bitcoin

In 2016, the market capitalization of Bitcoin reached over 10 billion USD [1], proving that designing and maintaining a distributed cryptographic currency is technically feasible today. Although the technical primitives, which are essentially cryptographic hash functions, and asymmetric cryptography have existed for a while, Bitcoin was the first concept to combine these technical building blocks with an incentive system, thereby creating the first *distributed* cryptographic currency in history. In this chapter, we describe Bitcoin as the archetype of modern distributed proof-of-work-based blockchains.

4.1   BITCOIN AT A GLANCE

Bitcoin and other related cryptocurrencies rely on two different types of data structures: *transactions* and *blocks*. Transactions are grouped together in blocks. The blocks are chained together via hashes of their predecessors, thereby forming an authenticated data structure, the *blockchain* [119]. Transactions and blocks are disseminated among all participating nodes using a gossiping protocol over a peer-to-peer (P2P) network.

A new block is added to the blockchain if a node of the network can provide a valid *proof-of-work* (PoW) for it. The PoW acts as a defense mechanism against Sybil attacks [60] and provides a form of *keyless signature* to authenticate new blocks as well as the blockchain as a whole [123]. Honest nodes agree that at any point in time only the longest blockchain is considered valid. Although commonly referred to as *longest chain rule*, it is actually the blockchain that is the hardest to compute in terms of PoW, i.e., the *heaviest chain*. If a node does not consider a block to be valid, then the block is not added to its blockchain. This *implicit consensus* process can be described as a "random leader election" on each solved PoW. The leader is allowed to propose a new block and implicitly agrees on all blocks before that by appending its new block to the end of the respective blockchain [119]. In short, Bitcoin can be described as a distributed system that uses PoW and a blockchain as a probabilistic consensus mechanism to agree on the contained set of transactions as well as their order. Thereby, the system ensures that all peers agree on the current ownership status of bitcoins. This is necessary to correctly handle state transitions in the ownership from one block to the next block. The underlying consensus approach to achieve this is referred to as *Nakamoto consensus*. Thereby, the leader is allowed to decide one block, then another leader is elected based on solving a PoW puzzle. The leaders signal their approval of previous blocks by appending to the rightful, in their view, chain of blocks. The probability of agreeing on a common prefix of blocks in the heaviest[1] chain increases toward $Pr(1)$ as the chains grows larger [76].

To motivate people to provide their computational resources and run Bitcoin nodes, so-called *miners* are rewarded with currency units (i.e., bitcoins) for every valid PoW provided for a block and its associated transactions.

As a result, the security and decentralization of Bitcoin comes not only from technical aspects but also from clever incentive engineering [119].

4.1.1   COMPONENTS OF CRYPTOCURRENCY TECHNOLOGIES

There exist multiple approaches to decompose cryptocurrency technologies. In [50] the authors describe cryptocurrencies by separating them into different *plains* like *network plane*, *consensus plane*, *storage plane*, *view plane*, and a *side plane*. Inspired by this approach, the authors of this book decided to decompose cryptocurrencies on a two-level basis. On the first level we introduce a rough separation into two main *components*. On the second level those two main components are decomposed into different *subsystems*. To avoid confusion with the "plains" concept defined in [50] or the "layers" of the OSI model we use the terms *components* and *subsystems* in this context.

The operation of Bitcoin and most other cryptocurrencies can be broken down into two main components: (I) *Consensus management* encompasses everything that is consensus relevant, e.g., consensus algorithms and communication aspects. (II) *Digital asset management* refers to all applications that build upon the agreed state and act upon it, e.g., key and transaction management. For a more fine-grained separation, both main components can be divided into multiple *subsystems*.

- Consensus management component

    - Network subsystem

    - Storage subsystem

    - Consensus algorithm subsystem

- Digital asset management component

    - Key management subsystem

    - Transaction management subsystem

With this separation into two main components, it is also possible to view such systems as distributed operating systems with applications running on top of them. In this analogy the consensus management component can be viewed as the operating system which provides services (e.g., syscalls) to userland applications, i.e., the digital asset management component. This view

---

[1] The heaviest chain is the chain containing the block with the hardest proofs-of-work.

highlights that both components can be replaced independently of each other. For example, if someone wants to use a different software for storing and using the public- and secret-key pairs related to her coins (i.e., a *wallet*) this would be possible without consensus critical changes. In other words, this would be the equivalent of changing the digital asset management component, which would not affect the other component as long as they can still communicate with each other, e.g., a wallet can run on any current instance of Bitcoin.

To the contrary, the subsystems within one component cannot be directly replaced without potentially influencing each other. For example, replacing the P2P networking implementation of Bitcoin with a different gossiping protocol would not directly touch the code on how to reach agreement, and hence the basic rules of Nakamoto consensus, however this change could alter message propagation times which in turn directly influence the achievable security and liveness properties of the consensus algorithm. Therefore, the subsystems are more contextualization to describe different parts more independently of each other.

Sections 4.3, 4.4, and 4.5 reflect this separation between *components* and *subsystems* and what they encompass in the context of Bitcoin as the archetype of modern distributed cryptographic currencies. To explain the inner workings of those subsystems in Bitcoin, several data structures are required, which are discussed in Section 4.2.

4.2   CORE DATA STRUCTURES AND CONCEPTS

Addresses, *transactions*, and *blocks* are the three basic data structures used in Bitcoin. The need for these specific data structures arose from the fact that Bitcoin was designed as a distributed digital currency. All cryptographic currencies that are based on Bitcoin, whether they are direct forks of it (e.g., Namecoin, Litecoin, Zcash) or just conceptually based on it (e.g., Ethereum), also include variants of these core data structures with some small modifications. This section describes those structures and shows how they interlink with each other to outline the basic concepts of a cryptographic currency. Because of the data-centric view of this Section 4.2, the details on how consensus is reached in Bitcoin is deferred until Section 4.3. For simplicity's sake, we assume in this section that the order of the blocks in the chain is agreed upon by every client and that each client knows at least the current head of the chain.

Over the lifetime of Bitcoin, there have been minor changes in the exact representation and interpretation of core data structures, e.g., the interpretation of the Version (*nVersion*) value of the block header, which originally just represented an increasing version number and is now interpreted as a bit vector so that miners can indicate whether they support features that require a soft fork. Most of the described constructs in this section have not been subject to major changes in the past.

In this section, we focus on the core components and fundamentals of the Bitcoin protocol in a generalized way irrespective of the exact protocol version. The information presented here is intended as a practical example to illustrate the general concepts of cryptographic currencies.

For up-to-date details, we recommend consulting the Bitcoin developer guide [23], the respective Bitcoin improvement proposals (BIPs) [24], and the source code of the reference implementation [22].

4.2.1   BLOCK

The most fundamental data structure in Bitcoin is a block. A block consists of a *block header* and the *transactions* associated with the respective block. These blocks are chained together by including cryptographic hashes of their predecessors to form a linked list commonly referred to as a *blockchain*.[2] The current state of currency is represented by the order of the blocks in the chain. They represent a ledger of all performed transactions, in which the transactions are processed sequentially depending on their position in the block in which they occur.

Block Header

Table 4.1 shows the different fields of the block header (80 bytes) and the associated list of transactions. The most important field of the block header from the integrity point of view is the *HashPrevBlock*. It contains a cryptographic hash (SHA256) of the previous block in the chain. This ensures that the blocks are chained together to form an immutable data structure. The integrity of this *blockchain* can be checked by anyone who has access to the head, i.e., the last block in the chain. A client that has stored only the last block can verify that the chain up to this point has not been altered. Therefore, he requests all previous blocks of interest and recreates the hash chain up to the last block. If the final block hash matches, no past blocks have been changed after their inclusion into the chain.[3]

Associated Transactions

The ordering of the list of transactions linked to every block is also vital, as they are processed in sequential order. This permits, for example, that the same funds can be moved several times by sequential transactions, all of which are associated with the same block.

All transactions associated with a block are tied to the respective block via a Merkle tree root hash that is included in the block header (i.e., *HashMerkleRoot*). For a simplified explanation, it is also possible to think of this field as a hash value over all transactions. If the content of one transaction would be changed after linking it to a block header, this would be detectable due to the change in the Merkle tree root hash.

4.2.2   BLOCKCHAIN

The term *blockchain*, although not directly introduced by Satoshi Nakamoto in the original paper [117], is commonly used as an umbrella term to refer to concepts related to cryptographic

---

[2]For a detailed definition of the term *blockchain* see Section 4.2.2.
[3]Although cryptographic hash functions always contain collisions, it is safe to assume that it is infeasible for an attacker to find them [6].

Table 4.1: Bitcoin block header (80 bytes) and its associated transactions (currently 1 MB) [122]

Field Name	Type (Size)	Description
nVersion	int (4 bytes)	Originally this specified only the version of the block. With BIP 9 coming into effect, bits of this field also indicate the support of features that require a soft fork [126].
HashPrevBlock	uint256 (32 bytes)	Double SHA256 hash of previous block header $SHA256^2(nVersion|| ... ||nNonce)$.
Hash MerkleRoot	Uint256 (32 bytes)	Merkle tree root hash (also called master or top hash) built from all transactions associated with the respective block.
nTime	unsigned int (4 bytes)	Timestamp in UNIX format of approximate block creation time.
nBits	unsigned int (4 bytes)	Target that defines the difficulty of the proof-of-work problem. This value is stored in a compact representation. For details see Section 4.3.3.
nNonce	unsigned int (4 bytes)	Nonce allowing variations for solving the proof-of-work problem.
#vtx	VarInt (1-9 bytes)	Number of transactions associated with the respective block. This field is not part of the block header but it is transferred along with the block over the network.
vtx[]	Transaction (Variable)	Vector of transactions that contains the actual data on them. These transactions are also not directly part of the block header but linked to it via the *HashMerkleRoot* field.

currency technologies. There are two common spellings throughout the literature for this term, i.e., *blockchain* and *block chain*. Although, the later variant was used by Satoshi Nakamoto in a comment within the original source code,[4] the first one has been used frequently in recent academic literature, e.g., in [50]. Therefore, we stick to this variant within this book. As with the spelling, there are also multiple definitions of the term *blockchain*. Therefore we provide two possible interpretations for this term in this book: (I) the *academic interpretation* and (II) the *colloquial interpretation*.

Academic Interpretation

Since multiple definitions of the term *blockchain* also exist in the academic context, this book outlines several of those interpretations. The first definition is a broad one that is independent

---

[4]https://github.com/trottier/original-bitcoin/blob/master/src/main.h#L795-L803

of the underlying consensus algorithm. Therefore it is applicable to all kinds of different types of blockchains and most accurately covers the broader usage of this term. We call this definition the *Princeton definition*, since it was first introduced informally in the Princeton Bitcoin book [119]. We provide this definition more explicitly in this section.

The second set of definitions is more formal and also includes consensus related aspects. They are the result of various approaches toward more formally modeling such systems and include works such as [77, 92, 93, 123]. These works do not necessarily define the term *blockchain* directly. Kiayias et al. for instance use the term *transaction ledger* for their definition in [93] while Pass et al. use the term *abstract definition* [123]. The evolution and details of these more formal analyses are outlined in Section 6.3.

For the remaining sections, up to but not including the entirety of Chapter 6, the *Princeton definition* as provided in [119] is sufficient to understand the concepts and follow the explanations.

Definition 4.1   A *blockchain*, according to the *Princeton Definition* [119], is defined as a linked list data structure, that uses hash sums over its elements as pointers to the respective elements.

By this definition, the construction of a blockchain ensures that as long as someone has stored or retrieved the correct block at the head of the chain, he is able to verify all other blocks of the chain when provided in their entirety.

Colloquial Interpretation

Colloquially the term *blockchain* refers to the category of distributed systems that are built using blockchain/cryptographic currency technologies, e.g., hash chains, asymmetric cryptography, game theory, etc. By this interpretation there exist two different versions of blockchains, namely: *permissionless* and *permissioned* blockchain.

permissionless blockchains   The central property of this type of blockchain is that the set of nodes, amongst which consensus over the state of the chain should be reached, is unknown. Vukolić et al. refers to this type as proof-of-work (POW) blockchains [147].

permissioned blockchain   The central property of this type of blockchain is that the set of nodes, amongst which consensus over the state of the chain should be reached, is known. Vukolic et al. refers to this type as Byzantine Fault Tolerant (BFT) blockchains [147]. Further distinction can be made between *permissioned* blockchains and *private* blockchain regarding the composition and selection of the set of nodes.[5]

4.2.3   ADDRESS

At the most basic level, Bitcoin addresses, like the addresses of many other cryptographic currencies, are cryptographic hashes of public keys. Therefore, each address actually consists of a

---

[5]https://blog.ethereum.org/2015/08/07/on-public-and-private-blockchains/

public and a private part. The public part is the address, which can be compared to an account number in ordinary online banking. The private part is the corresponding secret key, which can be compared to the password or signature required to withdraw money from an ordinary savings account. Addresses can be generated by anybody as easily as public/private key pairs. This allows everyone to accept Bitcoins by handing out the public address without any deeper knowledge of the Bitcoin protocol itself or its consensus mechanisms.

In Bitcoin, addresses are an Elliptic Curve Digital Signature Algorithm (ECDSA) [37] public/private key pair. More precisely, Bitcoin uses the elliptic curve *secp256k1* specified and recommended by Certicom [38]. To create a human-processable Bitcoin address, the public part is encoded as described in Algorithm 4.1. In the process, the public key is hashed multiple times. Thereby, two different hash functions are used, i.e., RIPEMD160 and SHA256 [121].

Algorithm 4.1 Construction of Bitcoin addresses from ECDSA public keys

---

Input : ECDSA public key *pk*
Output : Bitcoin address $\mathcal{A}$ e.g., 1DR8mXZpK75q7Vipkb1tmp8Wyjz6gDHZBL

1: $a = $ 0x00 || RIPEMD160(SHA256 (pk))
2: $h = $ SHA256(SHA256(a))
3: $\mathcal{A} = $ Base58(a || $h[251 : 255]$)

During this process, a 4 byte checksum is added at the end. The final result is then encoded with base58 encoding. A reason for the choice of base58 is that some base64-encoded characters are potentially visually indistinguishable in certain fonts, e.g., $\{0, O, I, l\}$. The source code snipped from Bitcoin Core[6] depicted in Listing 4.1 also highlights the reasons for choosing base58 encoding.

Listing 4.1: Comment on base58 encoding in base58.h of Bitcoin Core

```
 1  /**
 2   * Why base−58 instead of standard base−64 encoding?
 3   * − Don't want 0OIl characters that look the same
 4   *   in some fonts and could be used to
 5   *   create visually identical looking data.
 6   * − A string with non−alphanumeric characters is
 7   *   not as easily accepted as input.
 8   * − E−mail usually won't line−break if there's
 9   *   no punctuation to break at.
10   * − Double−clicking selects the whole string as
11   *   one word if it's all alphanumeric.
12   */
```

---

[6]https://github.com/bitcoin/bitcoin/blob/v0.13.1/src/base58.h#L6-L13

4.2.4   TRANSACTION

Transactions are used to transfer currency units from one address to another. They can be created by any entity that is in possession of currency units, i.e., bitcoins. Possession in this context means *control over the private key* of the respective address (i.e., public key) that currently holds the currency units that are to be transferred, i.e., an address that has received transactions in the past.

A transaction in Bitcoin consists of one or multiple *inputs* and one or multiple *outputs*. An input unlocks a previous output by providing a valid cryptographic signature. Thereby, the inputs serve as proof that the holder of the respective Bitcoin address that previously received the bitcoins is also in possession of the required private key. The private key is needed to generate the signature that unlocks the funds so that they can be used, i.e., transferred to another Bitcoin address.

For example, if *Alice* wants to transfer 5 bitcoins to *Bob*, she first requires Bob's Bitcoin address. For our example, we assume that this address is transferred over some trusted communication channel, e.g., displayed as payment information while shopping on a website that uses a valid certificate for TLS encryption [55]. Alice places Bob's address in the output of the transaction she is constructing together with the number of coins she wants to transfer to this account, i.e., 5. In the next step, Alice needs to prove that she is in possession of the required number of bitcoins and that she really wants to transfer them to Bob. Therefore, Alice searches the blockchain for previous transactions where bitcoins were sent to addresses that are under her control, i.e., where she is in possession of the corresponding private keys. She then unlocks as many of these previous transactions as needed to cover the desired output of 5 bitcoins. In our example, she uses two previous transactions (outputs) for this, consisting of 4 and 3 bitcoins. Referring to the respective previous transactions, Alice creates an input in the current transaction for every output she wants to unlock. These inputs uniquely identify previous outputs by their transaction ID and number. To unlock those outputs, she has to prove that she is the rightful owner, which she does by providing cryptographic signatures along with every input. Alice now adds an output to the transaction which transfers 5 bitcoins to Bobs Bitcoin address. Since the two unlocked inputs sum up to more than the desired value of 5 bitcoins, Alice adds another output for transferring the change of 2 bitcoins back to a Bitcoin address that is under her control. As soon as the transaction is constructed, Alice broadcasts it to the Bitcoin peer-to-peer network and waits until it is included in a newly generated block. Once the transaction is included at the head of the blockchain, the transaction is called *confirmed*. The number of confirmations is defined by the number of blocks that build on top of the block that contains the transaction.

Transaction Validation

Generally a transaction in Bitcoin is considered valid if the following criteria hold:

- All unlocked inputs have not been spent (i.e., unlocked and used) in a previous transaction.

- All cryptographic signatures in the inputs are valid.

- The sum of all values unlocked in the inputs is greater than or equal to the sum of all values specified in the outputs of the transaction.

For a more detailed description of check criteria, the reader is referred to the source code and the developer documentation [22, 23].

Coinbase

The above example transaction between Alice and Bob illustrates the general functionality of moving funds in Bitcoin, but it does not describe where bitcoins are actually created. This happens in the so-called *coinbase transaction*, which is the first transaction in every block and has a special status among all other transactions. In the coinbase transaction, the block creator is allowed to create a predetermined number of bitcoins out of thin air as a reward for finding a valid proof-of-work.

Figure 4.1 shows the structure of a block and the transactions it encompasses, with the first being the coinbase transaction.

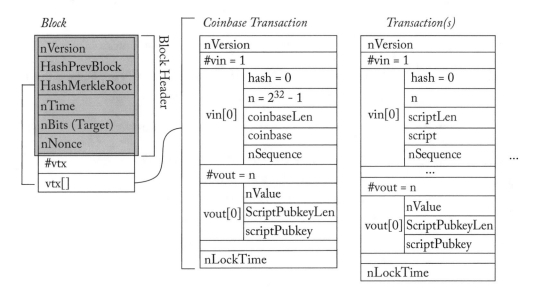

Figure 4.1: Data structure of block and the transactions it encompasses.

Table 4.2 highlights the exact differences between ordinary transactions and coinbase transactions.

Table 4.2: Difference between regular transaction and coinbase transaction structure [122]

Field Name		Type (Size)	Description
nVersion		int32_t (4 bytes)	Transaction format version (currently 1).
#vin		VarInt (1-9 bytes)	Number of transaction inputs entries in *vin*. For coinbase this is set to 1.
vin[]	hash	uint256 (32 bytes)	Fixed double-SHA256 hash of previous tx. For coinbase set to 0.
	n	uint32_t (4 bytes)	Fixed transaction output index. For coinbase set to $2^{32} - 1$.
	scriptSigLen or coinbaseLen	VarInt (1-9 bytes)	Length of *coinbase* or *scriptSig* field in bytes.
	scriptSig or coinbase	CScript (Variable)	The coinbase encodes the block height and arbitrary data (100 bytes max).
	nSequence	uint32_t (4 bytes)	Transaction input sequence number.
#vout		VarInt (1-9 bytes)	Number of transaction output entries in *vout*.
vout[]	nValue	int64_t (8 bytes)	Amount in Satoshis, 10^{-8} BTC. For coinbase this is the block reward plus transaction fees.
	scriptPubkeyLen	VarInt (1-9 bytes)	Length of *scriptPubkey* field in bytes.
	scriptPubkey	CScript (Variable)	Script specifying conditions under which the transaction output can be claimed.
nLockTime		unsigned int (4 bytes)	Timestamp until which transactions can be replaced before block inclusion.

Fees and Change

The amount associated with a specific Bitcoin address cannot be split up and has to be unlocked as a whole in a transaction input. Therefore, it is necessary to include additional outputs in a transaction if the surplus of currency units is to be transferred back as change to a Bitcoin address which is under the control of the sender.

If the sum of the values in the inputs of the transaction is still greater than the sum of the values in the outputs of the transaction, then this difference is collected as a transaction fee by the miner of the block in which the transaction is included. All transaction fees of a block are added to the reward of the coinbase transaction.

Scripts

As indicated in Table 4.2 and Figure 4.1 the transactions do not simply provide the required cryptographic signatures to unlock funds. Instead Bitcoin uses a stack-based non-Turing-complete scripting language (without loops) [23]. This so-called *Script* is split up into two parts. The first part resides in the transaction output that is to be spent (i.e., transferred), whereas the second part is given in the respective transaction input that is to unlock this fund. For the evaluation, both parts are concatenated and executed. If the execution returns *true* as a result on the stack, the script is considered valid and the respective fund is allowed to be spent in the associated transaction. Figure 4.2 shows an example execution of a standard Pay-to-Public-Key-Hash (P2PKH) transaction input that verifies that the rightful holder of the coins wants to initiate this payment. This example illustrates the status of the stack at each step of the execution from left to right. The script code that is executed contains a mixture of data (e.g., <sig>,<pubKey>,<pubKeyHash>) and opcodes (e.g., OP_DUP,OP_CHECKSIG,OP_HASH160,OP_EQUALVERIFY). When a data item is read from the script it is pushed to the stack. When an opcode is read from the script it is executed. In Figure 4.2 the stack depicts the execution state *after* the opcode, or data item, that is shown below the stack snapshot was processed.

Bitcoin scripting language example execution of P2PKH:

scriptPubKey (locks output)

| <sig> <pubKey> | OP_DUP OP_HASH160 <pubKeyHash> OP_EQUALVERIFY OP_CHECKSIG |

scriptSig (unlocks output within input)

				<pubKeyHash>		
		<pubKey>	<pubKeyHash>	<pubKeyHash>		
	<pubKey>	<pubKey>	<pubKey>	<pubKey>	<pubKey>	
<sig>	<sig>	<sig>	<sig>	<sig>	<sig>	true
<sig>	<pubKey>	OP_DUP	OP_HASH160	<pubKeyHash>	OP_EQUALVERIFY	OP_CHECKSIG

Figure 4.2: Example execution of a Pay-to-Public-Key-Hash (P2PKH) Bitcoin script in one transaction input.

4.3 CONSENSUS MANAGEMENT

This subsystem contains all consensus-critical parts, i.e., the rules on which the majority of the participating nodes have to agree to eventually reach consensus on the state of the blockchain. In other words, if there is an agreement on the validity and order of the blocks in the chain, then there is also an agreement on the order of transactions. This is required to determine whether a certain transaction is valid, i.e., uses only transaction outputs that have not been spent so far.

The randomized consensus in Bitcoin is based on proof-of-work to randomly select one node in the network to be the leader for the next "round" (i.e., the next block). The leader is allowed to propose the next block, then another leader is chosen according to the same principle and so forth. Following this process, the current leader can implicitly agree with the chain collected previously by appending his newly created bock at the head of the chain or disagree by choosing a different, i.e., previously created, block to append to. The chance of a node being selected as leader is dependent on his relative hashing power in comparison to all other nodes. Therefore, any node can increase its chances to be selected by increasing its computational share. According to current estimates,[7] this mechanism can be considered secure against a malicious node participating in the consensus as long as his share does not increase above 25% of the overall hash rate. This value resembles a current estimate and is the result of a still ongoing process of modeling and assessing the security guarantees of PoW blockchains [79] under certain attacks [67, 69] and combinations thereof [120]. In addition to the random selection, the proof-of-work also acts as protection against *Sybil attacks* [60] in Bitcoin. This is necessary since nodes can join (and leave) the Bitcoin P2P network and start (or stop) participating in the protocol at will.

From that perspective, the proof-of-work ensures that an attacker actually needs the respective computational power to generate new blocks and hence directly influence the consensus process.

In this section, we discuss the basic properties of proof-of-work and how the *mining* process in Bitcoin is organized. We also cover and briefly explain the adjustment of the proof-of-work hardness in Bitcoin and the difference between *target* and *difficulty*. Finally, we discuss the security guarantees and corner cases like *blockchain forks* and *double spending*.

4.3.1 THE IDEA OF PROOF-OF-WORK (POW)

The idea[8] of performing and providing a proof-of-work (PoW) for security reasons was developed and refined by Dwork et al. [63], Back [10], and Finney [70]. The history as well as some of the first implementations and use-cases of proof-of-work schemes are summarized in [10]. To introduce the concept of hashcash we outline an example for hashcash-based throttling [10] that we call *hashslash*. Hashslash is based on the same principles but slightly deviates from other implementations. In hashslash, the PoW was intended to ensure that it would be computationally hard for a spammer to transmit mail over an anonymous mail relay [10, 63]. Since the identity of the sender is to be protected, no authentication checks are possible in such a scenario. Therefore, the mail server required the solution to a computational challenge as an authentication method before it would accept the message for relaying.

---

[7]For details refer to Section 4.3.7.
[8]See Chapter 3 for context.

In hashslash, this is realized via an additional e-mail header line. The SHA1 hash value of this header line had to start with a given amount of zero bits; only then would the header be considered a valid proof-of-work. A regular client that wanted to transfer an e-mail had to find a *nonce* value for the header such that the SHA1 sum of the entire header line started with the required number of zero bits. Listing 4.2 shows a valid example solution where the nonce value is set to 369. In addition to the requirements for the outcome of the hash function, the header also had to comply to the following structure:

- Version information (1).

- Number of leading zero bits, i.e., target (12).

- UNIX timestamp (1231002905).

- Recipient e-mail address (satoshin@gmx.com).

- Random value to avoid reuse of proof-of-work (rluN7en).

- Counter or *nonce* that is incremented to find a valid solution.

Listing 4.2: Proof-of-work in hashslash

```
$ echo −n "1:12:1231002905:satoshin@gmx.com::rluN7en:369" | sha1sum
000c2c9c9e601fa2aef6eb80c9d6f2361f99f6a4
```

The brute force search for this example shown in 4.2 can be accomplished within one line of bash script as shown in Listing 4.3. In this specific instance of hashslash, a solution can be found on average after $\approx 2^{12}$ tries. For details on how to calculate the probability of finding a solution see Section 4.3.2.

Listing 4.3: Finding a valid PoW for hashslash

```
$ for i in {1..10000}; do echo −n "1:12:1231002905:satoshin@gmx.com::rluN7en:$i" |
    sha1sum | grep "^000" && echo "i=$i"; done
```

4.3.2 PROOF-OF-WORK IN GENERAL

A proof-of-work (PoW) in the context of computer science is a mechanism that enables a *prover* to provide evidence to a *verifier* that he has invested computational resources (e.g., CPU and memory) into a certain task. There are different definitions and requirements regarding the construction of such proofs [44, 63, 83, 142]. We focus on the aspects relevant in the context of cryptographic currency technologies. In this domain, these types of puzzles are sometimes also called *hash puzzles* [119], *computational puzzles*, *moderately hard puzzles*, or *scratch-off puzzles* [109]. On an abstract level, the main characteristics that a PoW, in the context of cryptographic currencies, has to fulfill can be summarized as follows:

1. Any given PoW is easy to verify.

2. The PoW is difficult to generate.

3. The difficulty of the PoW is parametrizable.

4. It should not be possible to reuse previously generated PoWs.

5. It should not be possible to generate PoWs ahead of time and use them later.

The first three are the basic requirements for a PoW, which are also highly relevant in other application scenarios. Requirements 4 and 5 are particularly relevant in the context of cryptographic currencies, as we will demonstrate in this section. To do this, we will first revisit our hashslash example outlined at the beginning of Section 4.3.1 and check whether it fulfills all of these requirements.

The requirements 1, 2, and 3 are fulfilled due to the properties of the underlying cryptographic hash function (see Section 2.1.1 for background). The PoW is easy to verify since any given PoW value is the result of the underlying hash function and hence can be verified by rerunning the hash function on the same input (easy to compute). The PoW is difficult to generate, i.e., only through brute force search, because it is infeasible to generate messages that correspond to a specific output of a cryptographic hash function (pre-image resistance). The difficulty of the PoW is parametrizable because there is a range of allowed hash values that are accepted as valid PoW. Expanding or reducing this range makes the PoW easier or harder.

The reuse of previously generated PoWs (4) is hindered by enforcing the structure of the header line on the server side. The header must contain a timestamp, the recipient, and a unique random value. Additonally, the server has to check the random value and confirm that it has not been used before. If this is the case, a valid PoW cannot be reused even for the same recipient address.

To minimize the storage requirement on the server for already used random values, the server can only save the random values for a certain timespan and discard every message that has an older timestamp as invalid.

Now let us see whether the last property (5) is also fulfilled by hashslash. Is it possible to generate valid PoW ahead of time and use them later? Yes, unfortunately it is possible to pre-generate arbitrarily many valid headers by simply setting the timestamp to the desired value in the future at which the messages are to be sent to the server. In this way, an attacker can pre-compute as many PoW as he wishes and use them at the desired point in time, flooding the server with valid messages. Although such an attack is theoretically possible, the attacker cannot avoid investing computational resources into computing those headers. Therefore, sending many spam messages is still a computationally intensive task.

Before we look at how this requirement is handled in cryptographic currencies, we first formally define the properties of a PoW in this context. Since this field is evolving rapidly, there are multiple definitions [109, 119]. We have decided to use the definition of a *hash puzzle* by Narayan et al. [119], because it is less generic and specifically tailored to Bitcoin-like PoW blockchains. As a result, it is also relatively simple.

Hash Puzzle: Taking the five stated requirements into account, we define a *hash puzzle* in accordance with Narayanan et al. [119], as outlined in 4.2:

Definition 4.2 A *hash* or *search puzzle* consists of:

- a cryptographic hash function $H()$.

- a random value r.

- a target set S.

A solution is a value, x, such that

$$H(r||x) \in S.$$

The random value r in this case is required to fulfill the properties 4 and 5 mentioned previously. In the context of hash puzzles, the pre-image resistance of a cryptographic hash function is extended by a hiding property. This is achieved by requiring a random number r so that is not possible to deduce the input x even if it has low min-entropy, e.g., is the result of a coin flip and either heads or tails. Even then it would be infeasible to determine the exact input to the hash function (i.e., if x is heads or tails) if r has high min-entropy.

In the case of cryptographic currencies, the random value r is required to avoid already calculated and used valid PoWs being reused and to ensure that PoWs are not calculated ahead of time by some miners. Therefore, r has to come from a source of randomness that is available to all participating miners. In Bitcoin, this is solved by enforcing a certain structure of the block header that includes a cryptographic hash value of its predecessor, i.e., the block that was created before the current one. With this construction, it is not possible to start mining, i.e., searching for a valid solution for the PoW, before the previous block has been created. Moreover, the structure of the block header also ensures that it is not possible to reuse valid old PoWs. For example, the timestamp is required to not be too far in the past or in the future. In addition, the value of the previous block hash, i.e., the previous PoW, is partially random since it is the output of a cryptographic hash function. In other words, if r is the result of a public source of randomness and not known beforehand then all properties required for a PoW are satisfied by the hash puzzle construction.

4.3.3 PROOF-OF-WORK IN BITCOIN

In this section, we describe in detail the structure of the PoW in Bitcoin and the relationships between the individual variables, like *required zero bits*, *nBits*, *target*, and *difficulty*. We also provide methods for estimating the required number of computations and thereby the hardness of the PoW.

Hash function $H()$:   Bitcoin uses two different cryptographic hash function constructions:

- **Main Hash:** $H_M(x) = \text{SHA256}(\text{SHA256}(x)) = SHA256^2(x)$

- **Address Hash:** $H_A(x) = \text{RIPEMD160}(\text{SHA256}(x))$

Since we are only interested in the PoW in this analysis, we define H as an instance of the *main hash*, which is calculated by invoking SHA256 twice on the input x that consists of the respective block header.

$$H(x) = H_M(x). \tag{4.1}$$

The value n often refers to the output length of the hash function in bits. For example for SHA256 $n = 256$. Then the number of possible outputs would be defined as:

$$n = 256$$
$$N = 2^n. \tag{4.2}$$

Required zero bits z: We use the variable z to refer to the number of required leading zero bits in $H(x)$ such that the output of $H(x)$ qualifies as valid. In other words, if $H(x)$ is in the target set S, then x is considered a valid PoW. Related work sometimes uses the variable t instead of z, but this can lead to confusion since t is often used to refer to time e.g., when calculating the mean time to find the next block. The smallest allowed value for the required number of leading zero bits in Bitcoin is $z = 32$. The biggest value that can be represented with the required number of zero bits z is $2^{n-z} - 1$.

The required zero bits are a simplified construction that is mostly of relevance when talking about rough estimates regarding the PoW in Bitcoin. For precise verification, the *nBits* value is used, which itself is a packed representation of the real *target*.

Target T: Every input x that produces an output $H(x)$ that is below or equal to a certain *target* value T is considered a valid solution to the PoW puzzle. Therefore, the target T defines the upper bound for the output of $H(x)$.

A proof-of-work as used in Bitcoin is based on a partial pre-image attack [81] on the cryptographic hash function SHA256 [121]. This process can be defined as finding a combination of a current block header and a nonce such that $\text{SHA256}(\text{SHA256}(blockHeader)) \leq T$. The *block header* of a Bitcoin block comprises (i) constraint variables that hold the required meta information (e.g., the hash of the previous block), (ii) variables that can be chosen with a certain degree of freedom (e.g., a Merkle tree root hash of transactions belonging to this block), and (iii) an arbitrarily-chosen variable (i.e., a nonce). The detailed structure is depicted in Figure 4.6.

The chaining of the $SHA256$ hash function, i.e., $SHA256^2(x)$, makes certain attacks less likely, but has little influence on the hardness of the PoW in general.[9] The input x to this function is the block header of a valid Bitcoin block. This block header also contains a *nonce* value that

---

[9]For details see Rasmussen et al. [81].

can be changed arbitrarily during this brute force search. Definition 4.3 shows the PoW validity criteria in Bitcoin.

Definition 4.3   A PoW in Bitcoin is defined as finding an input value x to the hash function $H()$ such that:

- x is a valid *block header* composed of meta data and a *nonce*, which can be changed arbitrarily during brute force search.

- the output of $H()$ is equal to or below the *target* value T.

$$x = \text{block header} = \text{meta data} \,\|\, \text{nonce}$$
$$H(x) = \text{SHA256}(\text{SHA256}(x)) = \text{SHA256}^2(x) \leq T.$$

For example, if you have a cryptographic hash function H with an output size of $n = 4$ bits and you require a proof-of-work with $z = 2$ leading zero bits, then you can check the validity of the proof-of-work as shown in Equation 4.3.

$$H(x) \leq 2^{n-z} - 1. \tag{4.3}$$

Listing 4.4: Example for checking condition in Python

```
1 >>> n = 4
2 >>> z = 2
3 >>> T = 2**(n-z)-1
4 >>> 0b0111 <= T
5 False
6 >>> int(0b0111 / (T+1)) < 1
7 False
8 >>> 0b0010 <= T
9 True
10 >>> 0b0011 <= T
11 True
12 >>> int(0b0011 / (T+1)) < 1
13 True
```

Thinking of the *target* T as a 256-bit value, it is clear that the number of leading zeros indicates the size of the set of valid solutions to the PoW puzzle. The higher the number of leading zeros, the lower the number of possible solutions, resulting in the PoW being harder to find. The maximum value possible for T, i.e., the easiest PoW, is defined in Bitcoin as $T_{\max} = 2^{224}$.

Difficulty D: The hardness of the Bitcoin PoW puzzle can also be expressed in terms of *difficulty*, defined as the ratio between the maximum target and the current target:

$$D = \frac{T_{\max}}{T_c}. \tag{4.4}$$

nBits: The *nBits*, *Bits*, or *compact* value is a packed 32 bit representation of the actual 256 bit target value. When the target value is calculated based on a given nBits value, it is called *derived target* or *target threshold*. Computing the derived target from a given nBits value and vice versa is not important for understanding the general functionality of PoW. However, since internally all calculations regarding the PoW in Bitcoin Core are based on the derived target, the required transformations might be of value to the practically inclined reader.

The following is an example for calculating the derived target T from an nBits value *30c31b18* stored in the block header. This value is stored in little-endian and therefore equals *0x181bc330* in big-endian. Listing 4.5 shows a summary of the required calculations taken from [23]. The calculation to derive the target works as follows:

1. Raw little-endian nBits value in block header

$$nBits_L = 0x30c31b18.$$

2. Raw big-endian nBits value in block header

$$nBits_B = 0x181bc330.$$

3. Select most significant bytes of *target* i.e., *Significant* or *Mantissa*.

$$T_{MSB} = 0x1bc330.$$

4. Multiply T_{MSB} with the *base* 256 squared by the exponent $0x18$ minus the number of bytes in the *Significant* i.e., 3

$$T = 0x1bc330 * 256^{0x18-3}.$$

Listing 4.5: Example for deriving target from nBits

```
1 nBits     = 0x30c31b18
2 nBits_be  = 0x181bc330
3 T         = 0x1bc330        *    256 ^ (0x18    -    3)
4
5           Significand            Base   Exponent    Number of bytes in significand
6           (Mantissa)
7
8 T         = 0x1bc3300000000000000000000000000000000000000000000000000000000000
```

Probability to Find a Valid PoW

The probability to find a value equal or below *target* T is defined as shown in Equation 4.5.

$$Pr(x \leq T) = \frac{T}{2^n}. \qquad (4.5)$$

If the target is solely defined by the required number of zero bits, then the probability can also be computed as shown in Equation 4.6

$$Pr(x \leq T) = 2^{-z}.\tag{4.6}$$

The probability of *not* finding a value equal to or below T is defined as shown in Equation 4.7.

$$1 - Pr(x \leq T) = 1 - \frac{T}{2^n} = \frac{2^n - T}{2^n}.\tag{4.7}$$

The probability of finding a value equal to or below T in y tries, i.e., the inverse of the probability of not finding a value equal to or below T in y tries 4.8.

$$Pr(x \leq T \text{ in y tries}) \approx 1 - (Pr(x \leq T))^y.\tag{4.8}$$

Equation 4.9 shows an approximation of the number of computations/tries that on average are required to find a value equal or below the target.

$$\frac{1}{Pr(x \leq T)} \approx \frac{2^n}{T} \approx 2^z.\tag{4.9}$$

4.3.4 MINING

Mining is the process of solving and disseminating PoW solutions as a means of reaching consensus on the current state of the blockchain. The nodes that are actively involved in searching and providing a solution to the PoW are called *miners*. The miners are rewarded with units of the mined cryptocurrency (e.g., bitcoins) as a compensation for their efforts and for investing computational power into the overall security of the cryptocurrency. Miners can join or leave the network at any time, increasing or lowering the mining power. Therefore, PoW blockchains need to adjust the PoW hardness so as to ensure that new blocks are generated at regular intervals. The higher the number T, the lower the number of possible solutions, resulting in the PoW being harder to find. The maximum value possible for T is defined in Bitcoin as $T_{\max} = 2^{224}$. This resembles 32 leading zero bits and, hence, an average number of 2^{32} tries to find a solution. As of December 2016, the current target is $T_c = 2^{224}/254620187304$. The current target requires approximately 2^{69} tries on average to find a solution. To sustain a block interval of approximately 10 minutes, a new target T_n is set every 2,016 blocks as a function of elapsed time t:

$$T_n = T_c * \frac{t}{2,016 * 10\text{min}}.\tag{4.10}$$

The probability of finding a new block is exponentially distributed and the mining rewards are paid out at irregular intervals, as the blockchain cannot account for all miners' actions while adjusting the difficulty. The mean time it takes to find a block (MTTB), i.e., a valid PoW, can be calculated depending on the share p of the total hash rate. When the block interval is 10*min* and you get a share of p percent compared to the total hash rate of the network, the mean time to the next found block is calculated as depicted in Equation 4.11.

$$MTTB = \frac{10 \text{ min}}{p}.$$ (4.11)

To generate a constant stream of revenue, miners team up and form *mining pools*, where they bundle their resources and share their rewards [102, 137]. The game theoretic aspects and the distribution of rewards in pooled mining were studied in [67, 102, 137]. Optimal strategies for mining pools have been discussed in the context of adversarial behavior and selfish mining [82, 120, 135].

Finite Supply

The smallest currency unit in the Bitcoin ecosystem is one *Satoshi*. One bitcoin is defined as $1 * 10^8$ Satoshis. The official currency symbol for bitcoin is XBT according to ISO 4217, but the community still widely uses BTC as symbol. It is a common misconception that the often-cited limited supply of 21 million bitcoin is ensured cryptographically. However, the artificial limit of 21 million bitcoins is established programmatically. As long as the majority of users obeys the rules defined in the reference implementation Bitcoin Core, the total number of bitcoins is limited to 21 million by the algorithm that issues the mining rewards. Every 210,000 blocks, a new era is reached and the received mining reward is halved. The algorithm defines 33 eras as depicted in Table 4.3.

Table 4.3: Eras of Bitcoin generation

Era	Reward	Date
1	50 BTC	2009-01-03
2	25 BTC	2012-11-28
3	12.5 BTC	2016-07-09
4	6.25 BTC	-
...	...	-
33	0.00000001 BTC	-

By setting the initial reward to 50 BTC (i.e., $50 * 10^7$ Satoshis), the overall supply of bitcoins s that can be created is defined as shown in Equation 4.12.

$$s = \frac{\sum\limits_{i=0}^{32} 210000 \lfloor \frac{5*10^8}{2^i} \rfloor}{10^8}.$$ (4.12)

4.3.5   BLOCKCHAIN FORKS

In the previous sections we described how mining works and how a PoW is calculated. The question remains: what happens if two miners find a block at almost the same point in time? In the following sections, we describe how PoW blockchains resolve such conflicts called *blockchain forks* and how attacks might utilize this resolution mechanism to perform *double spending* attacks.

If two miners find a valid block at approximately the same point in time, due to network latency they cannot know of each other's blocks. As a result both of them would start disseminating this block within the Bitcoin P2P network. In such a case, the nodes in the network are confronted with two different blocks that should be appended to the blockchain at the same block height, i.e., at the same point in the chain. A block that is not valid by the criteria defined for PoW, or well formed, for example by including invalid transactions, would immediately be rejected by an honest client and not disseminated further in the P2P network. However in case of an accidental blockchain fork both blocks simply represent valid but possibly different viewpoints of the current state of the network. For example, the blocks might contain different transactions since some of them have not reached both miners yet, or the transactions are in a different order. Moreover, both miners rightfully claim the respective block reward for this block since they provide a valid PoW for it.

Since the whole purpose of distributed cryptographic currencies is to ensure a total ordering of transactions and mitigate double spending attacks, only one of any concurrent set of valid blocks can be appended to the main chain. Valid blocks that have not made it into the main chain are referred to as *stale blocks*.[10]

The resolution of conflicting valid blocks is again based on the properties of PoW. Currently the reference implementation suggests that the miners decide randomly on which of the valid blocks they want to base their next block in the chain. Previously the reference implementation generally picked the block they received first, but for security reasons described in Section 4.3.7 this mechanism has been changed to the aforementioned random behavior. Basically miners are free to decide on top of which block they mine and until the next block has been found both conflicting blocks are considered equally valid. As soon as the next valid block is found one of the competing blocks has a successor and therefore becomes part of the *longest chain*. The more miners decide to extend the blockchain based on the same block the more computational power is aimed at finding a PoW that considers said block as a predecessor and therefore it is more likely that this block will be part of the main chain. This so-called *longest chain rule* ensures that such conflicts are resolved. More accurately, it is in fact not the longest chain but rather the chain that was the hardest to compute, i.e., the one with the highest cumulative difficulty. This ensures that an attacker cannot easily create a valid longest chain that primarily consists of blocks with a very low difficulty. Figure 4.3 shows a visual representation of a successful resolution of a blockchain fork. In this case there is a blockchain fork at block height

---

[10]Informally sometimes the expression *orphaned block* is used in this context, although in a strict sense this is incorrect [23, 68]. A *orphaned block* is a block that currently has no parent in the main chain (longest chain). This situation can happen while downloading blocks in the Bitcoin peer-to-peer network when block n is downloaded before block $n - 1$.

$n + 1$, where two valid blocks b_{n+1} and b'_{n+1} exist. Those blocks contain the same transactions x and y but in a different order. Despite some possible differences regarding some values in the block header (e.g., *nonce* and *timestamp*) the main difference between these blocks is in the coinbase transactions $t_{n+1,1}$ and $t'_{n+1,1}$ which rewards different miners for the creation of the respective block. As soon as block b_{n+2} gets mined and distributed the conflict is resolved and block b'_{n+1} is considered a stale block.

Real-world measurements on the stale block rate of the bitcoin network over a limited amount of time in late 2015 revealed a stale block rate of approximately 0.41% based on 24.000 Bitcoin blocks [79].

It should be noted that the stale block rate does not provide information on the concrete cause for why a block has become stale. This might be due to an accidental blockchain fork, or for example due to a targeted double spending attack (see Section 4.3.6). Even so, the stale block rate is an interesting metric that can serve as an indicator toward the security and reliability of proof-of-work blockchains but must be considered in the context of the particular protocol design. For instance, protocol modifications that may take stale blocks into consideration, such as Greedy Heaviest-Observed Sub-Tree (GHOST) [139], can help improve security properties in the context of high stale block rates, by allowing faster block intervals.

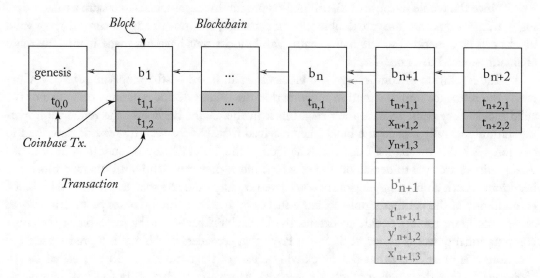

Figure 4.3: Blockchain conflict resolution in case of a blockchain fork.

4.3.6 DOUBLE SPENDING

In a central system double spending can easily be detected since there is only one central entity that is responsible for accounting. In the domain of distributed cryptographic currencies the mitigation of double spending attacks is a core problem. The remaining section illustrates how such attacks are mitigated in Bitcoin and other PoW-based cryptographic currencies.

Let us assume an example scenario where *Malory* wants to launch a double spending attack in the Bitcoin ecosystem. Generally speaking a successful double spending attack would allow Malory to spend the same units of currency twice. To execute the attack Malory requires some funds, which she can try to double spend and a merchant that accepts Bitcoin in exchange for goods. For our example, let's assume that *Alice* is a merchant who runs an exchange service on which she accepts bitcoins in exchange for U.S. dollars (USD). In a double spending scenario the goal of Malory is to convince Alice that she has received the required number of bitcoins, so that she sends out the equivalent number of USD in exchange, while convincing the rest of the Bitcoin network that this transaction to Alice has never happened. To achieve this, Malory creates two conflicting transactions that both reference the same *unspent transaction output* (UTXO). For our example it is enough to know that a Bitcoin transaction is composed of a variable number of *inputs* and a variable number of *outputs*. Each input unlocks the output of a previous transaction that has not yet been spent, i.e., unlocked. For more information, please refer to Section 4.2.4 where we have described the transaction format in greater detail. On a high level, a transaction in Bitcoin is valid iff:

- all its inputs have not been spent yet, i.e., belong to the set of UTXOs;

- the sum of all currency units (Satoshis) unlocked in the inputs is smaller than or equal to the sum of Satoshis in the outputs; and

- the Script program code in all inputs evaluates correctly, i.e., all provided cryptographic signatures over this transaction are correct.

If two transaction inputs reference the same transaction output of a previous transaction, only one of them can be valid. Malory generates two contradicting transactions x and x' that reference the same UTXO and are therefore mutually exclusive. Transaction x is designed to legitimately pay Alice, whereas x' transfers the same funds that should pay Alice back to Malory. Then she launches her attack and initiates the desired purchase with Alice. Thereby, we distinguish between three simplified cases:

Zero confirmation attack: In this case Alice sends out the goods, i.e., USD, immediately after receiving the unconfirmed transaction in the Bitcoin network. Since the transaction has not yet been included in a block it has *zero confirmations*. In such a scenario Malory can launch a successful double spending attack by transmitting the transaction x containing the correct payment directly to Alice's server in the Bitcoin network if she is able to deduce its IP address. At the same point in time she can disseminate the contradicting transaction x' to the rest of the network. This contradicting transaction is configured to transfer the same UTXO to another account/Bitcoin address which is also under the control of Malory. By distributing x' she increases her chances that this transaction will be included in a block first and thereby gets confirmed by the network instead of x.

One confirmation attack: In this case Alice waits until the transaction in question x is confirmed once, i.e., is included in a block (b_{n+1}) at the top/head of the blockchain, before she sends out the goods. To successfully perform a double spend attack Malory requires a blockchain fork that resolves toward block b'_{n+1} instead of b_{n+1} which includes the transaction x'. Figure 4.4 shows a successful double spending attack for this case.

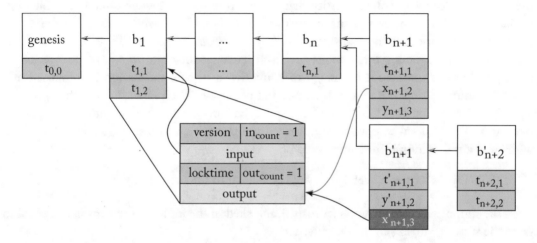

Figure 4.4: A potentially successful double spending attack on a merchant that only waited for one confirmation block.

n confirmation attack: Conceptionally this kind of attack is similar to the *one confirmation attack*, but in this case Alice waits for one or more confirmation blocks depending on the value of the transaction in question. The more confirmation blocks she waits for the longer a contradicting fork must be to allow for a successful double spend attack. This is the best strategy Alice can use to be secure against double spending attacks. In [79, 141] the authors describe such a scheme depending on the value(s) of the transaction(s) in question. While it should be noted that Bitcoin relies on probabilistic consensus and therefore in principle there is no 100% (i.e., *deterministic*) guarantee that a double spending attack will not work, regardless of the number of required confirmation blocks, the chances for a successful attack drop exponentially with the number of confirmation blocks [92, 134].

Figure 4.5 shows the probability for a successful double spending attack as it was estimated originally by Nakamoto [117] and Rosenfeld [134]. These estimates however do not consider *block withholding* attacks like *selfish mining* [69], or *eclipse* attacks [87] as well as combinations thereof termed *stubborn mining* [120].

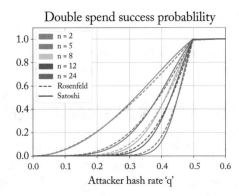 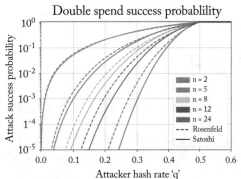

Figure 4.5: Success rate for double spending attacks depending on the hashrate of the attacker according to Nakamoto [117] and Rosenfeld [134]. Probability in linear scale (left) and logarithmic scale (right). The colors represent different numbers n of confirmation blocks.

4.3.7   DOUBLE SPENDING SUCCESS PROBABILITY

The security properties of Bitcoin are based on the assumption that the majority of the overall mining power belongs to honest miners. Early work in Bitcoin security modeling concluded that the mining power of all the honest miners has to be strictly greater than 50% so as to sustain the security of the blockchain [108, 117, 134]. If dishonest miners have the majority of the mining power, they can control the insertion of new transactions in the blockchain and the transaction fee market, hence, the supply of newly mined coins. In other words, all properties of a distributed system designed to work without a trusted third party are replaced by a mining monopoly.

More recent works found attack strategies that can be successful even without controlling the majority of the mining power. Examples include the *block withholding* [69] attacks like *selfish mining* [135], *eclipse attacks* [87], as well as combinations thereof termed *stubborn mining* [79, 120]. These attacks relate to information dissemination and aim to isolate portions of the network and partition it in disconnected clusters. By withholding or otherwise suppressing information propagation of newly generated blocks, malicious nodes can trick honest participants into "wasting" their computational power by mining on stale or older blocks that already have successors. This can give the attacker a disproportionate success rate of having their generated blocks be part of the eventually agreed-upon heaviest chain, while blocks generated by honest nodes are more often discarded in a losing fork. The success probability of such attacks increases with the mining power share (α) and the level of connectivity (γ) of the attacker. Below a certain bound for these parameters, honest mining outperforms these attack strategies. A poorly connected attacker ($\gamma \approx 0.1$) requires an $\alpha \geq 0.33$ to successfully perform selfish mining attacks [120]; an attacker connected to half of the nodes ($\gamma \approx 0.5$) would need an even lower $\alpha \geq 0.25$. Therefore, 25% is currently considered a conservative lower bound on the required mining power for an attacker to gain an advantage using these attack strategies over honest behavior.

For a more formal description of the security model of Bitcoin and Nakamoto consensus see Chapter 6.

4.4   NETWORK AND COMMUNICATION MANAGEMENT

This subsystem is related to the underlying communication mechanisms as well as the structure and characteristics of the peer-to-peer network. In this context, it is important to distinguish between different entities in the network. Whenever the term *node* is used, we refer to some entity that is actively participating in the consensus protocol, i.e., a miner. Thereby, we follow the nomenclature used in the literature on distributed systems. When we use the term *peer* or *client*, we are more generally referring to any interconnected entity within the peer-to-peer network of the currency or an entity that is at least trying to establish a connection to this network. This might be a miner or a client program that does not participate in the consensus or does not have a full copy of the blockchain, e.g., an SPV[11] wallet.

The Bitcoin and cryptographic currency community do not necessarily care about this distinction when using the term *node* or *peer*, but since we will also describe distributed systems aspects in Chapter 6, we require a more fine-grained separation of terminology. The term *full node* is used when we refer to some entity that is not necessarily participating in the consensus protocol by mining blocks but is at least forwarding messages within the peer-to-peer network and storing a full copy of the blockchain. Although this wording might be misleading regarding our definition of *node*, we opted to adhere to the nomenclature used in the cryptographic currency domain in this context.

Since PoW blockchains like Bitcoin can be characterized as *online systems*, they require a connection to other peers, at least from time to time, so that they can synchronize on the current state of the blockchain. In Bitcoin, information is disseminated and collected in the underlying P2P network via a gossiping protocol. This protocol and the underlying network structure and characteristics it produces are outlined in this section. We will avoid going into too much detail and describe everything at a higher level for the following reasons: (i) Over the lifetime of the bitcoin reference implementation, the networking subsystem has undergone some changes. Some of these changes were introduced to increase performance, while others were supposed to mitigate security or privacy flaws and harden the system. (ii) The details of the networking and communication subsystem are not necessarily relevant for the security of the consensus system as long as some basic properties regarding synchrony are fulfilled. For the consensus algorithm it is important that the propagation delay between nodes that are currently online is low compared to the block creation interval [12, 50, 51]. Generally speaking, the used consensus algorithm im-

---

[11]SPV stands for Simplified Payment Verification and describes a process for verifying the validity of transactions without storing a full copy of the blockchain.

poses some constraints (or requirements) on the underlying communication system. For details see Chapter 6.

4.4.1 SEEDING AND CONNECTING

The first step when initializing or starting a peer-to-peer client is a discovery process to find peers it can connect to. This process is called seeding. When a client is started for the first time, there is no past information on already known peers that could be retried, i.e., reused in connection attempts. Therefore, a seeding mechanism is required that can also bootstrap new clients. The Bitcoin reference implementation *Bitcoin Core* uses the following seeding scheme to find other peers that are currently online. There are between 5,000 and 10,000 Bitcoin peers online that accept connections [50, 110].

1st check for old peers: Initially, the client tries to connect to already known hosts that it collected in a previous session. In doing so, it uses some ranking scheme based on several factors that are not described in detail here. In general, the decision whether or not to attempt a connection to a specific IP address is influenced by: (i) the time elapsed since it was notified about this IP, (ii) whether it has already been connected to it, (iii) the subnet in which the IP address resides. This should prevent a client only connecting to IP addresses in one subnet that are under the control of the same entity.

   If the Bitcoin Core client is started with the `--connect=<ip>` option, then the IP specified there is the only IP it will try to connect to. This may be useful for someone running their own trusted server that they like to use for other clients.

2nd check DNS seed server: If the client has not yet been connected to other peers or was offline for a long period of time, it uses DNS servers to query a list of currently active peers. The DNS servers / DNS names are hardcoded into the client software and return a set of approximately 250 IP addresses in a round-robin fashion.

3rd fallback: If all above-mentioned methods fail, a client has some hardcoded IP addresses of well-connected peers that can be used as a fallback. Moreover, it is possible to add peers manually before invoking the client via the `--addnode=<ip>` command line option.

   As soon as a client is connected to a remote peer, it can query this peer for IP addresses of other clients. Each peer keeps an address pool, i.e., a list of addresses of other clients to which it has recently been or is currently connected. The maximum number of connections a client can have is 125 inbound plus outbound.[12] This constant can be changed by invoking the client with the `--maxconnections=<n>` option. Generally, clients try to keep active connections to eight other peers and, therefore, allow 117 incoming connections. The limit for the number of

---

[12]cf. Bitcoin Core source `https://github.com/bitcoin/bitcoin/blob/a55716abe5662ec74c2f8af93023f1e7cca 901fc/src/net.h#L78`.

outgoing connections cannot be changed directly with an option on startup.[13] Therefore, if a client is positioned behind a router that performs network address translation (NAT), it is only connected to eight other peers. There are two methods by which connected clients can exchange information about other peers.

- GETADDR: A client can request messages from other peers it is currently connected to via a GETADDR message. As a result, it receives mostly about 1,000 addresses.

- ADDR: In special cases, a client can receive unsolicited ADDR messages containing IP addresses.

4.4.2   NETWORK STRUCTURE AND OVERLAY NETWORKS

Theoretically, the Bitcoin peer-to-peer network should form a random graph, but empirical analysis by Miller et al. shows that there exist high-degree vertices/peers with 70 to 708 connections [110]. Moreover, they found that two percent of the reachable peers account for three-quarters of the mining power in Bitcoin. Besides the publicly reachable peers, there is an unknown number of peers that resides behind NAT. Those clients are mostly short lived and connect to the network from time to time. More information on the Bitcoin peer-to-peer network can be found in the following publications [21, 51, 80, 87, 140].

In addition to the peer-to-peer network, there is a fast overlay network now called *bitcoinfibre*.[14] This network was formally known as *Bitcoin relay network* or referred to directly by the name of the key maintainer Matt Corallo. The purpose of this overlay network is to establish fast connections between miners to exchange information about new blocks in a timely manner. This is intended to prevent blockchain forks that are caused by a high network-induced delay between miners.

4.5   DIGITAL ASSET MANAGEMENT

This subsystem encompasses everything that is related to key and transaction management, for example:

- Creating and storing public private key pairs, i.e., usable addresses.

- Creation, tracking, and bookkeeping of transactions.

- Management of different accounts with distinct balances.

- Keeping a history of all transfers.

---

[13]cf. Bitcoin Core source https://github.com/bitcoin/bitcoin/blob/a55716abe5662ec74c2f8af93023f1e7cca901fc/src/net.h#L62.

[14]cf. Homepage http://bitcoinfibre.org/.

The described functionality is covered by tools that are usually referred to as *wallets*. To date, a huge variety of tools is available for managing bitcoins and for interacting with the Bitcoin ecosystem. As they can logically provide different functionality and offer different security or usability benefits, they pose significant challenges for their users. Chapter 5 provides an overview of coin management tools and discusses their implications on user experience based on the findings from a large-scale user study.

4.6 ALTCOINS

4.6.1 NAMECOIN AND MERGED MINING

Namecoin [2] is an alternative cryptocurrency (i.e., an *altcoin*) derived from Bitcoin. It was the first fork of Bitcoin and, hence, the second distributed cryptocurrency in history. Besides being a cryptocurrency, Namecoin intends to provide an alternative to the Domain Name System (DNS) and offers the possibility to store arbitrary name-value pairs in its blockchain. The underlying design of Namecoin is heavily based on Bitcoin but extends the Bitcoin protocol by introducing *transaction types*, which introduce a structured approach toward handling the storage and management of additional information in the blockchain (e.g., DNS entries).[15]

Merged Mining
Merged mining was originally conceived as a bootstrap technique, aiming to increase the PoW difficulty and, as a consequence, the security of altcoins in their early stage, when they are more vulnerable to dishonest miners. Merged mining aims to improve the blockchain security by rapidly increasing the number of nodes participating in the distributed consensus. The key idea of merged mining is to allow a blockchain (e.g., Namecoin) to accept valid PoW produced for another blockchain (e.g., Bitcoin), provided that they meet the hardness criteria of the receiving (child) blockchain even if they do not meet the criteria of the sending (parent) blockchain.

Merged mining was first implemented in Namecoin. By accepting Bitcoin blocks through merged mining, Namecoin quickly achieved a high difficulty level. Thanks to this, Namecoin still has the highest mining difficulty of all Bitcoin-derived altcoins.Other popular altcoins, including Litecoin and Dogecoin, have already adopted merged mining, establishing it as a *de facto* hardening mechanism for altcoins.

The implementation of merged mining has not been without controversy. There are already discussions on realistic threats on network centralization[16] and scam attacks.[17] Merged mining has been neither sufficiently documented nor studied in the literature until now. The

---

[15]With Bitcoin it is also possible to use OP_RETURN opcodes to store arbitrary information in the Blockchain, but these methods are not well standardized.

[16]cf. `https://www.cryptocompare.com/mining/guides/what-is-merged-mining-bitcoin-namecoin-litecoin-dogecoin/`.

[17]cf. commentary on the Eligius CoiledCoin scam, available on `https://bitcointalk.org/index.php?topic=56675.msg678006#msg678006`.

work described in the next sections aims to fill this knowledge gap and provide a systematic study of the actual effects of merged mining on the security of altcoins.

The most detailed textual description of merged mining to date is provided as a Bitcoin Wiki entry [118]. The only additional information available is the source code of the merged mining implementation in the various altcoins. We analyzed all these sources of information and provide in this section a systemized description of merged mining and its data exchange formats.

A parent blockchain *must* support a method to link to or include some arbitrary data in its block headers. This data comes from the child blockchain. For most of the PoW blockchains, this requirement is fulfilled using the structure of the *coinbase transaction*, depicted in Figure 4.6.

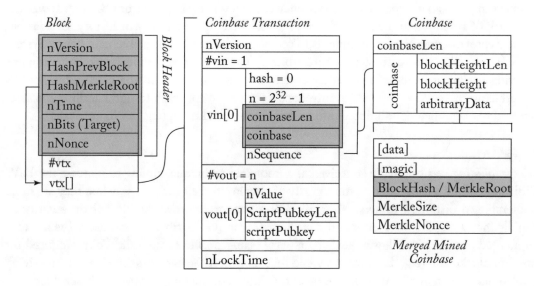

Figure 4.6: Common PoW blockchain data structures.

The coinbase transaction is a special type of transaction for rewarding the block miner. It comprises *n transaction outputs* (denoted as vout[0]), which transfer the mined coins to the account(s) of the miners, and one special *transaction input* (denoted as vin[0]). This special input includes the "block reward" (denoted as nValue) and the "coinbase" fields. The *block reward* comprises new cryptocurrency units that are created up until the maximum supply is reached (currently this is set to 12.5 for Bitcoin). The *coinbase* encodes the current *block height* and can contain up to 96 bytes of arbitrary data, as summarized in Table 4.4.

The last 40 bytes of the coinbase field can be used to store information for the child blockchain. If merged mining involves only one child blockchain, then 32 bytes define a BlockHash, i.e., the hash of the block header of the child blockchain directly. If more than one child blockchain is involved, the 32 bytes form the MerkleRoot, i.e., the root hash or a

Table 4.4: Structure of the coinbase of a merge-mined block. Uses Namecoin as an example [118].

Field Name		Type (Size)	Description
coinbaseLen		VarInt (1-9 bytes)	Length of the `coinbase` field in bytes as a variable length integer. Maximum size is 100 bytes.
coinb.	blockHeightLen	(1 byte)	Length in bytes required to represent the current `blockHeight`.
	blockHeight	(3 bytes)	Current block height.
	[data]	char[] (0-52 bytes)	Optional: Arbitrary data that can be filled by the miner (e.g., identifying the block miner).
	[magic]	char[] (4 bytes)	Optional: If *len(coinbase)* ≥ 20, `magic` bytes indicate the start of the merged mining information, e.g., "\xfa\xbe".
	BlockHash or MerkleRoot	char[] (32 bytes)	Hash of the merge-mined block header. If more than one cryptocurrency is mergemined, this is the Merkle tree root hash of those cryptocurrencies.
	MerkleSize	uint32_t (4 bytes)	Size of the Merkle tree, i.e., the maximum number of contained cryptocurrencies.
	MerkleNonce	uint32_t (4 bytes)	Used to calculate the indices of the mined cryptocurrencies in the Merkle tree. If no Merkle tree is used, it is set to 0.

Merkle tree of size `MerkleSize`. The leaves of the tree represent the hashes of the block header of each child blockchain.

It is vital to ensure that merged mining does not occur for multiple forks of the same child blockchain; this would compromise the security of the latter. This is addressed as follows: Each child blockchain has a fixed `chainID` that is hard-coded in its client implementation and is defined by its developers. For example, the `chainID` for Namecoin is set[18] to the value `0x0001`. Every miner can choose freely for how many and for which PoW child blockchains they want to perform merged mining and, hence, maintain a different Merkle tree. The combination of `MerkleSize`, `MerkleNonce`, and `chainID` are fed to a linear congruential generator so as to produce the unique position of a child blockchain `chainID` on a Merkle tree of a given size.[19]

---

[18]cf. Namecoin source code on https://github.com/namecoin/namecoin-core/blob/fdfb20fc263a72acc2a3c460b 56b64245c1bedcb/src/chainparams.cpp#L123.

[19]cf. Namecoin source code on https://github.com/namecoin/namecoin-core/blob/fdfb20fc263a72acc2a3c460b 56b64245c1bedcb/src/auxpow.cpp#L177-L200.

4.6.2   OTHER EXAMPLES

Litecoin [129] forked from Bitcoin by replacing its PoW. Litecoin uses the *scrypt* cryptographic hash function, which is considered to be memory-hard [127]. The aim was to reduce the advantage of Bitcoin miners using hardware devices (ASICs) specifically built for high-performance SHA256 hash operations. Litecoin uses a reduced block interval of 2.5 minutes.

Dogecoin [56] started as a toy experiment but is now maintained by a vibrant community. It is an indirect fork of Litecoin with a smaller block interval of one minute and a slightly adjusted difficulty and reward algorithm over time.

CHAPTER 5

Coin Management Tools

In this chapter, we discuss current practices and tools for managing digital assets, as well as associated security, privacy, and usability implications, and future research and design strategies.

Bitcoin users have an enormous variety of tools to choose from when it comes to managing their digital assets. In the Bitcoin terminology, such tools are currently referred to as *wallets*, following the metaphor of a traditional currency. Originally, a wallet was defined as a collection of private keys.[1] Hence, anything from a mental representation of a private key to a dedicated software can be considered a wallet. To avoid misconceptions and because this definition of a wallet is very narrow, we have introduced the broader definition of a *Coin Management Tool* (CMT) [98] to account for the other areas without which most cryptocurrencies would not work. A CMT refers to a tool or a collection of tools which allows users to manage one or more core tasks of a cryptocurrency. In particular, the network and blockchain layer of Bitcoin and other cryptocurrencies is not only important for the integrity of the system as a whole, but has a significant impact on the security and privacy of each and every end user.

Most of the currently available tools referred to as wallets provide functionality beyond storing keys, such as performing Bitcoin transactions and downloading parts of the blockchain. Contrary to other public key crypto-systems, e.g., PGP/GPG, Bitcoin is not fully communication-channel agnostic. In the case of Bitcoin, the interaction with the Bitcoin network is an integral part of operating in the distributed system. In contrast to other signing systems, Bitcoin tools need to keep state information on performed transactions and account balances.

Even though there is a great variety of software available for managing bitcoins, users still need to deal with the technical fundamentals and perform backups so that they can recover their virtual monetary assets in case of a loss. Therefore, these systems are not resilient to human errors and have a variety of potential attack vectors. Reports from online forums and mailing lists show that many Bitcoin users have lost money due to poor usability of key management and security breaches such as malicious exchanges and wallets.

5.1 HISTORY AND CATEGORIZATION OF CMTS

In this section, we discuss and categorize CMTs by the degree of control and verifiability a user can exercise with a designated client. The proposed scheme is tailored to Bitcoin-like cryptocurrencies, but expressly designed in the most generic way possible so that it can be applied to other

---

[1]https://en.bitcoin.it/wiki/Wallet

derived cryptocurrencies as long as their design is not fundamentally different. The categorization according to our scheme makes it possible to quickly distinguish clients by their underlying capabilities. From a user's point of view, knowledge of these underlying models is crucial for making an informed decision regarding the level of trust they can put into an individual client.

When Bitcoin was in its infancy, *bitcoind* was the only available Bitcoin client which performed all required tasks: *mining management, P2P network communication and blockchain management, key management,* and *virtual asset management.* With the growing popularity of Bitcoin and cryptocurrencies in general, more and more software was developed which focused on a subset of individual tasks of the original implementation. Moreover, the design of Bitcoin allows users to use it even if they are not running mining software or a full P2P client (full node). As a result, there are software implementations with varying feature sets in which the handling of public-private key pairs is the most sensitive and, therefore, the most common core feature. A CMT for example might cover every task of a cryptocurrency except for mining management. This definition should not indicate the need to include the full functionality in every client software but account for the diverse feature sets required to operate a cryptocurrency and, at the same time, avoid the ambiguity of the term "wallet."

To categorize CMTs, we first identified critical CMT tasks which are directly related to security and privacy issues. This covers aspects of key management, like generating keys/addresses and signing transactions, and P2P network communication and blockchain management, like handling connections and verifying and storing the blockchain. These core tasks can be used to divide CMTs into five categories. A client can fulfill the requirements of more than one category depending on its configuration.

- **Basic Client:** A client which runs on a user-controlled device and can perform key management operations, but cannot perform any P2P network communication. Therefore, it is not a stand-alone solution. This category includes some dedicated *hardware clients/wallets* and *cold-storage* clients which require a second online device for transaction processing.

- **Fully Functional Basic Client:** A client which runs on a user-controlled device and performs all P2P network communication and blockchain verification-related tasks, keeps a copy of the full blockchain, can perform all key management-related operations, and executes the mining algorithm. In other words, this is a client which can perform all tasks required to operate a cryptographic currency (e.g., the Bitcoin core implementation *bitcoind* when the option *setgenerate true* is set).

- **Thick Client:** A client which runs on a user-controlled device and performs all P2P tasks related to network communication and blockchain verification, keeps a copy of the full blockchain, and can perform all key management-related operations. This type of client is sometimes referred to as *thick client* or *full node.*

- **Thin Client:** A client which runs on a user-controlled device and performs certain P2P tasks related to network communication and blockchain verification but does not keep a copy of the full blockchain, although it can perform all key management-related operations. This type of client is sometimes referred to as *thin client* or *mobile client/wallet* and includes so-called SPV clients/wallets (Simplified Payment Verification), e.g., Electrum.

- **Hosted Client:** A client which does not run on a user-controlled device and where all tasks are performed by a trusted third party on behalf of the user. This type of client is sometimes referred to as *hosted* or *web client/wallet*. In this case, it is not relevant whether key management is handled in the browser (e.g., via JavaScript) since this would require the user to download and verify the script code from the website of the third party every time they want to use it.

5.2 METAPHORS

As Bitcoin is considered a currency, the use of related metaphors seems natural and, from a naive perspective, intuitive. In the Bitcoin ecosystem, the metaphors of traditional currency are broadly used to describe and perform actions with a client, such as sending/receiving coins. Even though the use of metaphors seems, at first glance, like a user-friendly way to communicate how the cryptocurrency can be used, it poses the risk of creating significant misconceptions, and fails in many ways.

According to Eskandari et al. [65], aspects of Bitcoin transactions fail because they do not easily fit the coin metaphor and conversely encourage users to overextend the metaphor, which can lead to confusion on the user side. In contrast to physical coins, bitcoins are exchanged neither physically nor virtually. Therefore, the coin metaphor fails in describing how transactions are handled. In the case of Bitcoin transactions, the private key must remain in the sender's possession and is solely used to sign transactions. As discussed by Eskandari et al. [65], the metaphor of *sending* bitcoins is misleading, as it only describes the process of digitally signing a transaction rather than an actual exchange of virtual units.

In the metaphorical cryptocurrency terminology as used by many CMTs, the role and purpose of public and private keys is insufficiently explained to the user and, therefore, creates misleading cognitive models. Furthermore, the role of the respective keys is not contextualized by the metaphor and not self-explanatory to the non-expert user. This poses significant risks of key loss or unintentional key sharing. We argue that this source of misconception needs to be addressed in future user-centric designs for CMTs. To date, the challenge of user-friendly key management remains unresolved and is still a subject of scientific research in the area of usable security.

5.3 USABILITY

We conducted a large-scale study with 990 Bitcoin users to understand security, privacy, and related coin management challenges in the context of user interactions with the Bitcoin ecosystem [98]. Our results suggest that users still struggle with finding the best trade-off between usability and security. In the following, we summarize the results of this comprehensive study, which was the first of its kind [98]. For our analysis, we collected both quantitative and qualitative data. The quantitative data were collected via an online questionnaire that was distributed via mailing lists and online forums to Bitcoin users, who received compensation for their time in (micro) bitcoins. The qualitative data were collected via open-text questions in the online survey and in additional qualitative semi-structured interviews to gain deeper insights and to explore reasons for phenomena observed in the online questionnaire.

5.3.1   BITCOIN MANAGEMENT STRATEGIES AND TOOLS

In the course of our study, we found that a significant number of Bitcoin users use solely web-hosted CMTs to manage their digital assets. The most popular CMT was Coinbase, followed by Bitcoin Core, Xapo, Electrum, and MyCelium. Only 35.5% of Coinbase users reported backing up their CMT. Hence, the remaining proportion of users shifted the responsibility to the CMT provider, which is paradoxical in terms of the philosophy of a decentralized system, but comprehensible from a usability and convenience perspective. In the case of lost keys or a security breach, however, it is arguable to what extent such digital assets are restorable.

In contrast to the behavior and backup morality of Coinbase users, 83.5% of MyCelium users reported that they back up their CMT. This is not surprising when we take a closer look at the backup procedure provided by MyCelium. Making a complete and secure paper backup is easy and convenient. The CMT allows users to print parts of their key on paper and then lets them fill in the remaining digits of the key. The qualitative interviews conducted by Krombholz et al. [98] confirm that the backup process is perceived as convenient and easy-to-use by tech-savvy and non-tech-savvy users. Our results as described in [98] also suggest that users of web wallets store a much smaller number of bitcoins in third-party-hosted CMTs.

Table 5.1 shows the most widely used Bitcoin wallets. The question permitted multiple answers, as it is common for users to have more than one wallet. The table also shows the number and percentage of participants in our sample who use a certain wallet. Furthermore, Table 5.2 shows whether users protect their wallets with a password and whether the wallets are encrypted. Our findings show that the majority of users protect their wallets with a password. In the case of web clients, we observed a lack of background knowledge. For example, 47.7% of Coinbase users in our sample said their wallet was encrypted and 34% said they did not know whether it was encrypted. We observed a similar trend for Xapo, which is the third-most used wallet in our sample. Just like Coinbase, it is also a web-hosted tool, and similarly to Coinbase, only about half the users say it is encrypted and about a third do not know whether it is encrypted. Regarding backups, only a third of Coinbase users and 43% of Xapo users back up their wallets. 33.9% of Coinbase and 28.5% of Xapo users do not know whether their wallet is backed up. We also found that Bitcoin users with more than 0.42BTC (100 USD) did not back up their CMT more often than users with fewer bitcoins. This effect is statistically significant in our sample ($\chi^2(1) = 5.1$, $p = 0.02$).

Table 5.1: Properties of the most frequently used wallets mentioned by our participants

CMT	Number	Percent	BTC
Coinbase	314	31.7	238
Bitcoin Core	236	23.8	752
Xapo	179	18.1	157
Electrum	125	12.6	226
MyCelium	97	9.8	62

Table 5.2: Properties of the most mentioned CMTs. The three blocked columns contain user responses (in percent) to whether the CMT is encrypted, whether it is backed up, and whether there is an additional backup (Yes, No, and I don't know (IDK)). The rightmost column contains the sum of bitcoins stored in a respective CMT by our participants.

CMT	Encrypted?			Backup?			Additional Backup?		
	Yes	No	IDK	Yes	No	IDK	Yes	No	IDK
Coinbase	47.5	18.5	34.0	35.5	30.6	33.9	30.3	66.9	2.8
Bitcoin Core	72.8	16.1	11.1	76.3	14.0	9.7	64.0	32.2	3.8
Xapo	51.4	19.0	29.9	43.0	28.5	28.5	41.3	57.5	12
Electrum	72.8	15.2	22.0	77.6	16.0	6.4	55.2	44.0	0.8
MyCelium	61.9	21.6	16.5	83.5	12.4	4.1	52.6	47.2	0.2

We also asked our participants whether they created additional backups in case their primary backup gets lost or stolen. In our sample, Bitcoin Core users had the highest rate of additional backups, with 64% saying they make a secondary backup of their wallet. Table 5.3 shows self-reported properties of wallet backups. According to our data, none of our participants stored backups on an air-gapped computer. The most reported backup properties were encryption and password protection. 197 backups were stored in a cloud.

59.7% of our participants use only one wallet to manage their bitcoins, 22.7% use two, and 10.6% use three wallets. The remaining 7% use four or more wallets. The maximum number of wallets a participant reported using was 14. This participant justified the high number by explaining that he wanted to try out different wallets before choosing those that met his requirements best. About half of our participants who used a web client did this exclusively to manage their bitcoins. The other half used a web client in addition to a local client. To our surprise, our results show that most coins of our participants are stored in Armory.[2] The Armory users in our sample have about 3,818 BTC in their Armory altogether, with the top five users reported to

---

[2]https://bitcoinarmory.com/

Table 5.3: Backup properties in absolute mentions in descending order; a user can have multiple wallets and multiple backups

Backup Properties	Mentions
My backup is encrypted.	662
My backup is password protected.	629
My backup is stored on external storage (e.g., USB drive).	430
My backup is stored on paper.	334
My backup is stored in the cloud (e.g., Dropbox).	197
My backup is stored on an air-gapped device.	0

have 2,000 BTC, 885 BTC, 300 BTC, 230 BTC, and 150 BTC. The highest reported number of bitcoins stored in a participant's web client was 100 BTC. The reported sum of all coins stored in Coinbase is 238 BTC, and 157 BTC in Xapo. Figure 5.1 illustrates the accumulated bitcoins per wallet as reported by our participants.

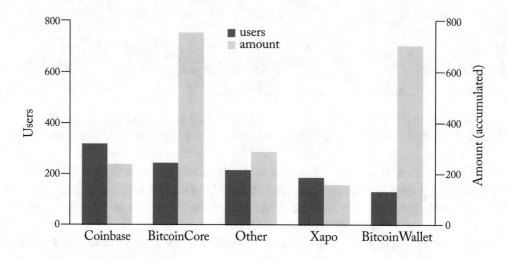

Figure 5.1: Self-reported wallet usage and accumulated hosted bitcoins per wallet.

5.3.2   ANONYMITY

We found that 32.3% of our participants believe that Bitcoin is anonymous per se when, in fact, it is only pseudonymous. 47% think that Bitcoin is not anonymous per se but can be used anonymously. However, about 80% think that it is possible to trace their transactions. 25%

reported having used Bitcoin over Tor to preserve their anonymity.

We also asked participants whether they took any additional steps to stay anonymous. 18% reported frequently applying methods for staying anonymous on the Bitcoin network. Most of them reported using Bitcoin over Tor, followed by multiple addresses, mixing services, multiple wallets, and VPN services. As shown by Biryukov et al. [20, 21], using Bitcoin over Tor creates an attack vector for deterministic and stealthy man-in-the-middle attacks and fingerprinting.

5.3.3 PERCEPTIONS OF USABILITY

Although most participants in our qualitative interviews were very much concerned about the security and privacy aspects of Bitcoin management, eight of the ten persons interviewed said that they would recommend web wallets and deterministic wallets to non-tech-savvy Bitcoin users, highlighting convenience and ease as the main benefits. One participant said that he would definitely recommend a wallet where the private key is stored on a central server to make key recovery easier and to obviate the need for comprehensive backups, and that mnemonics would help. Six participants also said that they would recommend MyCelium[3] as the most usable wallet. Those who had already used MyCelium consider the paper backup procedure the most usable and secure form of backup. To create a paper backup with MyCelium, the user has to print out a template that contains some parts of the key and then fill in the empty spots manually. Some participants expressed initial discomfort when they used paper wallets.

Most interviewees also highlighted the need for fundamental education in early years of childhood. P2 said that Bitcoin is inherently complex, that the fundamental idea of public key cryptography should be taught in school, and that monetary systems are a matter of culture.

Two participants also highlighted that user interfaces should be simplified and minimalized. Many participants stated that for a fast proliferation of Bitcoin, simple and intuitive UIs are more important than security. They argued that computers proliferated, even though most people do not know how computers work and that security is not necessarily an argument when it comes to large-scale adoption. They provided examples such as cars in the 1940s, computers, credit cards, and WhatsApp. They also said that the amount of money that is circulating in the Bitcoin network is low enough to take the risk of losing it and compared this scenario to the risk of losing cash. Some participants also proposed a dedicated device with an intuitive UI for key management and think that such an artifact would be the most secure and usable option.

5.4 USER EXPERIENCES WITH SECURITY

Usability challenges potentially have an impact on the security experience. When using a decentralized currency, users are responsible for managing their digital assets. Hence, in case of a security breach, they are responsible for recovering their keys in order to prevent monetary loss.

---

[3]https://mycelium.com/

In the following, we report user experiences with security breaches and their ability to recover from them.

About 22.5% said that they had lost bitcoins or Bitcoin keys at least once. Of these, 43.2% said it was their own fault (e.g., formatted hard drive or lost a physical device with Bitcoin keys), 26.5% reported that their loss was caused by hardware failure (e.g., a broken hard drive), followed by software failure (24.4%; e.g., keyfile corruption) and security breaches (18% e.g., malware, hacker).

The majority (77.6%) of those who lost bitcoins did not want to say whether they were able to recover their keys. Of those who provided an answer, 65% were not able to recover their keys. In total, our participants reported to have lost about 660.6873 bitcoins. However, it must be taken into account that we did not ask when the coins were lost. Given that the Bitcoin exchange rate is highly volatile, it is hard to provide an overall estimation in USD. About 40% of our participants reported to have lost money due to a self-classified major security breach. 13.1% of our overall sample reported to have lost bitcoins in HYIPS (*high-yield investment programs*) and pyramid schemes. 7.9% lost money at Mt. Gox.

We also gave our participants the opportunity to describe how they dealt with the incident. Most participants stated that they did not do anything to recover their keys and simply accepted the loss. Some argued that the financial loss was not worth the effort to take further steps or that they felt helpless and did not know what to do. Those who actually took action most frequently mentioned that they filed claims and contacted the exchange or online wallet provider. Those who lost money to a malicious online wallet reported switching to other types of wallets instead of hosted/online wallets. The participants who lost money in HYIPS mostly stated that they started to use less risky investments and learned from their previous mistakes. Irrespective of the security breach, many participants reported to have spread the word over forums on the Internet and shared their experiences with other affected users.

Eight participants in our qualitative interviews reported that they had experienced an intentional or accidental key and/or Bitcoin loss. Three participants were affected by the Mt. Gox security breach and two of them reported to have filed a claim on Kraken.[4] One participant reported having lost a *physical* Casascius[5] bitcoin but stopped searching for it as it was only worth about 9 USD at that time. Others also mentioned having lost their keys due to device failure, corrupted HDDs, or software failure.

Krombholz et al. [98] also investigated user perceptions of risks associated with Bitcoin. We provided the participants with 11 risk scenarios. We selected the risk scenarios based on findings from scientific literature and evidence from online resources. For each risk scenario, we provided an easy-to-understand description and asked the participants whether they thought the risk was likely or unlikely to occur. Figure 5.2 shows the participants' risk estimation. Our results show that the participants consider value fluctuation to be the highest risk, followed by

---

[4]https://www.kraken.com/
[5]https://www.casascius.com/

vulnerabilities in hosted wallets and Bitcoin theft via malware. Our participants estimated the risk for cryptographic flaws as the lowest, followed by double-spending attacks and DoS attacks on the Bitcoin network.

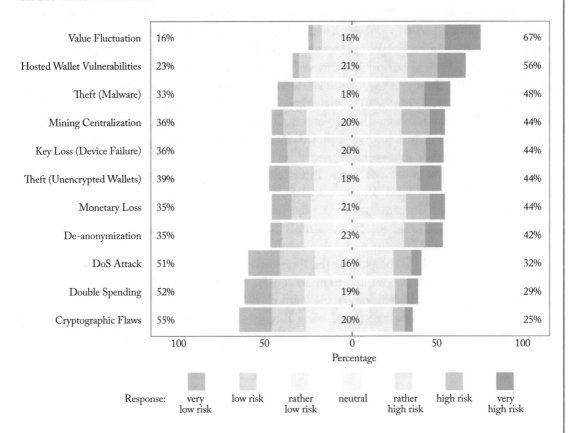

Figure 5.2: User perceptions of risk scenarios in percentage of participants ($N = 990$).

5.5   CRYPTOCURRENCY USAGE SCENARIOS

Most participants reported using Bitcoins for tips and donations (38.0%), followed by virtual goods, such as web hosting, online newspapers (33.3%), online shopping (27.5%), altcoins (26.5%), gambling (26.5%), and Bitcoin gift cards (19.9%). About 5% reported buying or having bought drugs with bitcoins. 30.2% of our sample reported using Bitcoin at least once a week, 25% stated that they use Bitcoin at least once a month and 19% at least once a day. The remainder of the participants said that they used Bitcoin once a year or less. These results suggest that the majority of respondents in our survey use Bitcoin frequently.

We also asked our participants about the number of bitcoins they were currently holding. About half the participants did not want to specify. According to those who did respond, our sample holds approximately 8,000 BTC in total. The majority of users (70%) started using Bitcoin between 2013 and 2015 and 17% started between 2011 and 2012. 58.0% reported using other cryptocurrencies in addition to Bitcoin, most frequently Dogecoin and Litecoin. The most popular Bitcoin exchanges in our sample are BTCE (20.9%), Bittrex (14.0%), and Bitstamp (13.0%). 11.4% of our participants are currently mining bitcoins. Most of them started mining after 2014. Many of those who started earlier have stopped mining as they currently consider it infeasible. 195 (19.7%) participants claimed to be running a full Bitcoin server that is reachable from the Internet. The top-mentioned reason for running a Bitcoin server was to support the Bitcoin network (60.5%), followed by fast transaction propagation (46.6%), network analysis (30.3%), and double-spending detection (26.1%).

All participants in our qualitative interviews were frequent Bitcoin users, and some of them are active in their local Bitcoin association. Most interviewees mentioned that the decentralized nature of Bitcoin was among the main reasons for them to start using Bitcoin. The second-most mentioned reason was simply curiosity. One participant, who used to live in Crimea at the time the Ukrainian-Russian conflict started, mentioned socio-political reasons. He was working for a U.S. company at the time and needed a safe and cheap option to receive his salary in Crimea. He also wanted to make sure he would not lose any money due to the annexation by the Russian Federation. In his opinion, Bitcoin was the best option, and according to him, many people in Crimea started using Bitcoin at the time. Some participants also used to mine Bitcoins some years ago, when it was still profitable to mine at a small scale.

CHAPTER 6

Nakamoto Consensus

While the utility and future potential of cryptocurrencies is relatively apparent, it may not be immediately clear why Bitcoin is proving to have a significant impact in the field of (distributed) fault-tolerant computing [147]. In this chapter we will therefore take a closer look at the principal mechanisms behind Bitcoin, or more precisely behind *Nakamoto consensus*, which can allow the system to reach eventual agreement upon the blockchain datastructure and its contents in the presence of potentially malicious actors from a distributed systems perspective and relate it to other research in the field of distributed computing.

6.1 THE PROBLEM BITCOIN STRIVES TO SOLVE

The governing principles behind Bitcoin have been dubbed[1] *Nakamoto consensus*, which builds on the combination of a distributed append-only ledger of digitally signed transactions called the blockchain, a cryptographic proof-of-work scheme that serves as a probabilistic consensus mechanism for agreement on the contents of this blockchain, and economic and game theory-based incentives for participants to uphold and enforce the protocol and consensus rules.

In order to gain a more effective understanding of why Nakamoto consensus presents a novel approach for addressing the problems of creating a system through which two willing parties can "*...transact directly with each other without the need for a trusted third party*" [117], it is necessary to relate it to various fundamental insights and research on distributed and fault-tolerant computing. Research centered around *Byzantine fault tolerance* is of particular interest, as Nakamoto consensus is part of this problem domain.

6.1.1 TRUSTED THIRD PARTIES

An essential property that separates Bitcoin and similar technologies from previous endeavors of creating electronic cash systems is its novel approach for solving the problem of having to place various degrees of trust in third parties. To prevent users from spending the same virtual currency more than once, generally referred to as *double-spending*, some form of global agreement needs to be reached on the ordering and state of transactions in the system. In its most basic form such an agreement may be provided through a single authority that validates new transactions and will reject any requests that are in violation of the defined guarantees. However, users of such a

---

[1]One of the earliest uses of the term can be attributed to N. Szabo in http://unenumerated.blogspot.co.at/2014/12/the-dawn-of-trustworthy-computing.html and has subsequently been used in publications such as [27, 104].

system need to place trust in that authority to uphold these guarantees at all times and not act maliciously.

Even if we only consider such a single trusted entity, a practical system would still require some degree of fault tolerance, where the failure of a single node does not render the service unavailable. Extending the model to multiple nodes is, however, no trivial task. Consistency between all the nodes of the system needs to be ensured in order to satisfy the previously stated property that users should not be able to spend the same currency units multiple times. One can easily envision scenarios, such as a partitioning of the network, that may enable a malicious entity to successfully perform a double-spend attack. Interestingly, in such a scenario a double-spend may be possible even if all the partitioned nodes remain honest. Clearly, providing a reliable and fault-tolerant *distributed* cryptographic currency is no trivial endeavor, even if one assumes a trusted third party.

6.1.2   PLACING TRUST IN A DISTRIBUTED SYSTEM

Above, we assumed a model where our digital currency system is comprised of a single trusted entity. But when such a system is extended to multiple nodes in order to improve fault tolerance, this actually implies that multiple entities can exist in which we have to place some amount of trust.[2] We should, therefore, treat our model as a distributed system with $\{p_1, p_2, \ldots, p_n\} = \Pi$ entities that we have to trust. Since our goal is to decrease the reliance on such trusted third parties, the next question might be whether and how the system could be augmented so that it can deal with a situation where a subset of the processes $\Pi' \subseteq \Pi$ can fail or act in a malicious way while still being able to uphold its defined guarantees.

The problem of ensuring a consistent state across multiple nodes where processes or their communication channels may fail has long been a subject of research in fault-tolerant distributed computing. Early outlines of this diverse research field have been given for instance by Christian [49] and Gärtner [78] and, as the name implies, its focus is aimed at the occurrence and handling of faults in distributed systems. The question of how to reach agreement in the presence of faults, in particular, is a fundamental problem [145] that has been the subject of much discussion since the problem was outlined by Pease, Shostak, and Lamport in 1980 [126]. Being able to reach agreement or *consensus* is an essential building block for developing fault-tolerant distributed systems. The results in [126] revealed that a surprisingly large number of nodes have to remain *correct* to be able to reach agreement,[3] if the faulty processes are allowed to deviate arbitrarily from their expected behavior. In this context *correct* implies that a process will not exhibit any faulty behavior for the entire duration of the execution.

As will later be outlined, this requirement on the number of correct nodes is strongly tied to the assumed system model and available primitives. Nevertheless, it was shown that

---

[2]Albeit under the command of a single authority.
[3]Specifically, they considered the *interactive consistency* agreement problem and found that ($n \geq 3f + 1$) nodes were required in the assumed system model.

distributed systems can be designed, where the need for trust can be distributed in a way that only requires a subset of all participants to behave correctly, while still providing relatively strong consistency guarantees. In this context trust can be considered a synonym for assuming the nonfaulty behavior of a node, while faults may imply potentially malicious behavior.

6.1.3   DECENTRALIZING TRUST

Bitcoin and its underlying mechanism for agreeing on the contents of the blockchain, namely *Nakamoto consensus*, extends the aforementioned model in certain key aspects. A variety of both conceptual and practical distributed systems exist that tolerate failures and malicious behavior in a subset of nodes and can provide primitives that are, in principle, suitable for building distributed ledger applications such as cryptocurrencies. These systems, however, generally assume a previously determined and fixed set of nodes which are actually responsible for reaching agreement, even if the total set of participants may be larger and can change over time [147]. Such a reliance on a predetermined group of consensus nodes can again raise certain concerns about trust, and while these systems may be considered *distributed*, they are not truly *decentralized*.

Through clever incentive engineering and a novel application of proof-of-work that prevents Sybil attacks and serves as a form of leader election, Bitcoin allows open and *anonymous participation* in the agreement process over the contents of the blockchain datastructure. Anyone can, in principle, participate in the Bitcoin protocol which presents a significant step toward a fully decentralized cryptocurrency system. At the same time this mechanism also promises to provide relatively strong resilience against faulty or malicious nodes and hence the problem of having to place trust in third parties. Because of the anonymous setting the resilience toward malicious participants is generally expressed in terms of their computational power or *hash rate*, that is, the number of valid PoWs all honest participants can produce in a unit of time in relation to those a malicious entity can generate.

Initially it was believed that Bitcoin could tolerate up to less than half (e.g., $< 50\%$) of the total hash rate being controlled by malicious entities at any time t, or more formally:[4]

$$\forall t : \sum_{b\in\mathcal{B}(t)} m(b) < \frac{1}{2} \sum_{p\in\Pi(t)} m(p), \tag{6.1}$$

where $m(i), i \in \Pi$ is used to denote the hash rate of process i and where $\mathcal{B}(t) \subseteq \Pi(t)$ is the set of malicious or *Byzantine*[5] processes, and $\Pi(t)$ the total number of (mining) processes, at time t. In this context multiple individual adversaries are treated as a single malicious entity because, in the worst case, they could collude.

This assumption has since been revised in light of various attack strategies, such as selfish and stubborn mining [69, 120, 135] and may be as low as $< 25\%$, i.e., at least $\frac{3}{4}$ of the hash rate needs to be controlled by honest participants at any time. Specifically, dishonest miners using

---

[4]Following the notation used by Eyal et al. in [68].
[5]The term *Byzantine* is explained in Section 6.2.2.

such strategies can achieve a situation in which a disproportionately large number of blocks relative to their hash rate will be included in the main (heaviest) chain, thereby greatly weakening some of the desirable properties of a proof-of-work blockchain. Modifications to the protocol have been proposed that may again strengthen its resilience to be able to withstand an adversary with up to less than 50% of the hash rate at any time [124] without a detrimental effect to the provided guarantees.

The concrete properties and guarantees that Bitcoin and Nakamoto consensus can provide are still an ongoing topic of research. We will outline relevant aspects of this area of research in the next Section 6.2, to give a better understanding of how Bitcoin relates to other work in the field of fault-tolerant distributed computing and where the potential strengths and weaknesses of Nakamoto consensus lie.

6.2   CONSENSUS AND FAULT TOLERANCE IN DISTRIBUTED SYSTEMS

The field of *fault-tolerant distributed computing* is relatively broad and covers a wide range of topic areas on how to provide reliable and failure-resilient systems. As was mentioned above, Bitcoin and similar cryptocurrency systems address the problem of having to rely on a trusted third party from a new angle by employing a novel consensus mechanism, namely Nakamoto consensus.

The topic of *consensus* is a distinct area of research in fault-tolerant distributed computing that deals with identifying the fundamental aspects of reaching agreement in a distributed system where processes and their means of communication may fail. Consensus is a fundamental building block for (reliable) distributed systems that can be used, for instance, to implement any *wait-free* concurrent data object among a set of processes [88] or serve as a basis for *active replication*, such as in the *replicated state machine* approach [100, 136].

In this section the focus is placed on fundamental aspects of consensus and *byzantine fault tolerance*. *Byzantine failures* can be *arbitrary* and potentially malicious and are well suited for describing the adverse environment in which cryptocurrencies such as Bitcoin strive to create a decentralized third party in which one has to place as little trust as possible. It will be outlined that Byzantine failures render consensus harder to achieve, and that properties of the assumed system model, such as its synchrony, greatly affect the solvability of consensus problems and may even render them impossible [73].

6.2.1   CONSENSUS

The term *consensus* is currently not well defined in the context of Bitcoin and blockchain technologies. It may be used when speaking about a social agreement, such as the Bitcoin community attempting to agree on future protocol changes, or refer to the governing rules of the protocol that determine whether a block is valid or not (sometimes called the *consensus layer* [103]). Within the field of distributed computing, however, the term *consensus* is generally used to refer to a specific problem or more accurately a class of problems that has its origins in seeking answers to the question of how to develop reliable and dependable distributed systems. In this context *distributed* does not necessarily imply large geo-spatial differences and could also refer to processors within a single system that communicate via message passing or distributed shared memory.

An obvious approach to increasing the resilience of such a system against (process) failures is to increase the redundancy. It is clear that in this case, in order to guarantee consistency, it is desirable that at any given point[6] any (active) non-faulty replica $p \in \Pi_c$, where $\Pi_c \subseteq \Pi$ is the set of *correct* processes, should agree on, and present to an external observer, the same state S_p, such that $\forall p, q \in \Pi_c, p \neq q \rightarrow S_p = S_q$.

The problem of processes being able to reach agreement on a value or set of values has been formalized as the *agreement* or *consensus problem* [71, 75] and is often defined through properties such as the following definition (6.1):

Definition 6.1   The *agreement* or *consensus problem* defined through three properties:

1. **Validity:** If a process decides a value v, then v was proposed by some process.

2. **Agreement:** No two correct processes decide differently.

3. **Termination:** Every correct process (eventually) decides some value.

The *Validity* and *Agreement* properties are referred to as **safety** properties because they guard against trivial solutions or solutions violating the desired consensus assumptions while the *Termination* property ensures **liveness**, i.e., that the algorithm eventually makes progress and produces some result. A trivial solution, for instance, would be a consensus algorithm that always outputs a predetermined value such as 1, no matter what values the processes actually propose. Such a solution would clearly satisfy the *Agreement* and *Termination* properties but is of little practical use.

These properties can, of course, be strengthened or weakened to cover different consensus problem classes. For instance, the *Agreement* property of Definition 6.1 can be further strengthened to require *uniform agreement*, resulting in the *uniform consensus* problem that is harder than consensus [40]. Uniform consensus requires that *all* processes, correct or not, decide on the same value.

Definition 6.2   Agreement property of *uniform consensus*:

2'. **Uniform Agreement:** No two processes decide differently

---

[6]The astute reader will interject that perfect synchrony, and hence strict consistency, is impossible to achieve in reality because communication is not instantaneous and local time drift exists. We may nevertheless consider such a desideratum and discuss what is achievable under certain system models and assumptions.

Consensus protocols terminate when all correct processes have halted. If this is achieved in the same communication round the processes are considered to have reached *immediate agreement*, otherwise they reach *eventual agreement* [71].

In its most reduced form, processes may only need to agree on a single binary digit, called *binary consensus*, i.e., the value $v \in V$ that a process can select as their proposal is in the set $V = \{0, 1\}$. Binary consensus is often encountered when formally describing or modeling consensus protocols and their properties [16, 72, 73] and can be transformed to *multivalued* consensus where the set of possible proposal values V can be arbitrarily large [116].

There exist various problems that are either variants of, or are closely related to, consensus, such as:

- Reaching agreement on a vector of values, either called *vector consensus* or referred to as *interactive consistency* [126], if agreement is also reached on whether participating processes are faulty.

- *Terminating Reliable Broadcast* (TRB) [85], where a distinguished *sender* from a set of processes is to disseminate a message to this set, so that all *correct processes* either agree upon the receipt of the message or that the sender is faulty.

- *The Byzantine Generals Problem*, which is actually a specific case of TRB where Byzantine failures are assumed [101].

- *Total Order Broadcast* (also referred to as *atomic broadcast*) [52], where messages sent to a set of processes are to be delivered by processes in the same *total order*.

- *The Group Membership Problem* (GMP) [132], where agreement by a set of processes is to be reached whether they belong to a particular group, and where additional processes may *join* as well as existing or failed processes may be removed or *leave* that group.

- *State Machine Replication* [136], where agreement is to be reached on both the input and its ordering to a set of replicated deterministic state machines, so that all replicas receive and process the same sequence of requests.

Some of these agreement problems have been shown to be equivalent to consensus, such as total-order broadcast, while others, such as TRB, may be harder [39].

The assumed *system model* plays an important part in the solvability and how these problems relate to each other. For instance, while consensus is considered to be a harder problem than reliable broadcast in an asynchronous system augmented with *unreliable failure detectors*[7] [39], adding the assumption of finite process memory to such a model actually reverses the case so that (single) consensus is easier to solve than reliable broadcast and repeated consensus is as difficult as reliable broadcast [54].

---

[7]The concept of unreliable failure detectors is explained in Section 6.2.2.

Early work on consensus was largely focused on agreement in the presence of arbitrary or so-called *Byzantine faults* [59, 101, 126, 130], but later, the topic of dealing with Byzantine failures, often referred to as *byzantine fault tolerance* or BFT, became a more distinct area of research.

The close relation between Byzantine consensus and Nakamoto consensus as well as its more distinct differentiation from other research on consensus warrant a more in-depth look at the topic of Byzantine fault tolerance, which is presented in Section 6.2.3.

6.2.2   SYSTEM MODELS AND THEIR IMPACT

So far, nothing has been said about important aspects of the system model such as the *types of failures* that can occur, or the *timing assumptions* for both processes and their communication links. The system model greatly influences how problems are solvable and even if a solution exists at all. Some of the outlined models and assumptions may strike the reader as being unrealistic or impractical and, at first, could appear to have little real-world relevance. For instance, assuming *asynchronous* communication between processes, that is, allowing an arbitrarily long delay between the sending and receipt of any message, does not appear to reflect the relatively strong synchrony of real-world communication links. Nevertheless, reasoning about a protocol under such an asynchronous communication model allows us to outline bounds and properties that do have practical relevance. For real-world systems, it is easy to envision situations where the assumed timing bounds do not hold, rendering synchrony assumptions probabilistic at best [39].

Assuming a system model that provides very weak guarantees may render a problem very hard or impossible to solve, while overly strong guarantees might allow for an easy solution, yet achieving these guarantees can become a hard problem in itself.

Synchrony Assumptions

One essential property of the system model that greatly influences the solvability of consensus are its *synchrony assumptions*. In their seminal work, Fischer, Lynch, and Patterson showed that reaching *deterministic* agreement in a system with asynchronous communication is impossible, even if message communication is reliable and only a single process can fail (in the crash-stop model) [73].

Effectively, without bounded delays on message transmission times, it is impossible to deterministically decide whether a process has failed or its messages have simply not yet arrived. To ensure that the *Agreement* property of consensus[8] under such conditions cannot be violated, the *Termination* property is no longer satisfiable, as a single failed process could require all correct processes to wait indefinitely for an answer.

This fundamental insight, which is commonly referred to as the *FLP impossibility result*, outlines an important limitation of all problems in the consensus domain. For real-world systems

---

[8]See Definition 6.2 in 6.2.1.

simply assuming stronger synchrony cannot fully address this issue, because components have a non-zero probability of failure, and hence also render such synchrony assumptions probabilistic.

Therefore, it is necessary to contemplate the possibility of timing failures and choose a suitable trade-off between availability and correctness, as no protocol can exist that deterministically guarantees both.

The FLP impossibility result has led to research on the minimal models of synchrony necessary to be able to reach consensus [58, 62].

Failures and Failure Detection

Above we have outlined that the synchrony assumptions of the system model play an important role in determining the solvability of consensus. At the core of the FLP impossiblity result lies the problem that one cannot reliably and deterministically decide if a process has actually failed or is merely slow to respond. To be able to reason about failures it is first necessary to define how the processes and communication links that make up the system can actually fail. After having done so one can then consider approaches toward the detection and handling of such failures within a particular system model.

A component is only considered to be *correct* if, during the entirety of an execution, it will not exhibit faulty behavior, else it is referred to as *faulty*. A protocol is considered to be f-*resilient* if it tolerates no more than f faulty processes of the n processes that make up the system. In related literature the variable t is also frequently used to represent faulty processes, hence t-*resilience* is also a commonly encountered descriptor. However, due to ambiguities, such as t also being regularly used to denote time, we will adhere to using f within this manuscript. The following definition (Definition 6.3) is a generalization of different failure types that can be encountered in the components of a distributed system.

Definition 6.3   Types of failures that processes and their communication links may exhibit:

- *Crash failure.* A basic failure model where components are assumed to crash and never recover.

- *Omission failure.* Here components may omit some actions such as sending messages or performing computations. Assuming the ability for processes to recover after a crash (*crash recovery*) also falls into this category.

- *Timing failure.* Timing failures occur when synchrony assumptions are violated. In an asynchronous system, this failure is irrelevant.

- *Byzantine failure.* Byzantine failures (sometimes also referred to as *arbitrary failures*) allow a component to deviate arbitrarily, and possibly maliciously, from its expected behavior. This includes duplicating or changing message contents, sending unsolicited messages, and temporarily or permanently exhibiting any of the previously listed failure characteristics.

Assuming Byzantine failures, in particular, can render consensus problems more difficult, as they allow faulty processes to deviate arbitrarily from their expected behavior. One way to address the underlying problem outlined by the FLP impossibility result, namely the inability to discern between a process that has crashed and one where it or its messages are merely very slow, is to query some form of *failure detector*.

Failure detectors are a form of *oracle* that a process can query and will provide a (possibly inaccurate) estimate on whether a process is believed to have failed or not. In 1996, Chandra and Toueg presented the concept of unreliable failure detectors which are characterized by a *completeness* and an *accuracy* property [39]. Here, instead of considering concrete synchrony assumptions, problems rely on a distributed failure detector abstraction that is based on local unreliable failure detector modules to determine whether a process has failed. Any concrete timing requirements are, therefore, moved into the actual implementation of the local unreliable failure detector modules, and problems can be expressed and classified purely through the abstract class of failure detector required to solve them.

Chandra and Toueg define eight different classes of failure detectors based on two completeness and four accuracy properties and show that the weakest class of failure detector required to solve consensus in asynchronous systems is $\diamond\mathcal{W}$, requiring *weak completeness* and *eventual weak accuracy*.

In contrast, terminating reliable broadcast, and hence the Byzantine Generals Problem, are shown to require a failure detector in $\mathcal{P}$, which exhibits *strong completeness* and *strong accuracy*.

A failure detector is considered *reducible* if a distributed algorithm exists that transforms failure detector D into D', written as $D \succeq D'$. If $D \succeq D'$ and $D' \succeq D$ then D is considered *equivalent* to D', written $D \cong D'$. Analogously, a class of failure detectors C is reducible to C' if $\forall D \in C, D' \in C' \rightarrow D \cong D'$, written $C \cong C'$ [39].

Definition 6.4 Failure detector properties used for their classification:

The *Completeness* properties are:

1. **Strong Completeness:** Eventually every process that crashes is permanently suspected by every correct process.

2. **Weak Completeness:** Eventually every process that crashes is permanently suspected by some correct process.

The *Accuracy* properties are:

1. **Strong Accuracy:** No process is suspected before it crashes.

2. **Weak Accuracy:** Some correct process is never suspected.

3. **Eventual Strong Accuracy:** There is a time after which correct processes are not suspected by any correct process.

4. **Eventual Weak Accuracy:** There is a time after which some correct process is never suspected by any correct process.

Table 6.1: Different classes of failure detectors

Completeness	Accuracy			
	Strong	Weak	Eventual Strong	Eventual Weak
Strong	Perfect $\mathcal{P}$	Strong $\mathcal{S}$	Eventually Perfect $\Diamond\mathcal{P}$	Eventually Strong $\Diamond\mathcal{S}$
Weak	$\mathcal{Q}$	Weak $\mathcal{W}$	$\Diamond\mathcal{Q}$	Eventually Weak $\Diamond\mathcal{W}$

Static and Dynamic System Models

For consensus problems, the distributed system is generally modeled as a bounded number of processes $\{p_1, p_2, \ldots, p_n\} = \Pi$, where communication between processes occurs by *message passing* over *reliable point-to-point links*. It is usually assumed that the communication graph is *bidirectional* and *completely connected*; however, work in the field has also addressed other topologies [57, 101], communication modes (such as distributed shared memory), and failure modes. Models where both the set of processes and their communication links remain static are referred to as *static distributed systems*. Interestingly, there is no commonly agreed upon definition for the *dynamic system model*, and research on consensus in such dynamic models is currently not as widespread. This situation may now change because Bitcoin and similar cryptographic currencies can be better described using a dynamic system model, providing further incentives to explore this topic area.

In Baldoni et al. [11] give the following informal definition and propose and investigate two attributes that such definitions should contain: "*a dynamic system is a continually running system in which an arbitrarily large number of processes are part of the system during each interval of time and, at any time, any process can directly interact with only an arbitrary small part of the system.*"

The first attribute [11] relates to the entities that may join and leave the system. An infinite arrival model is assumed where, in each run, infinitely many processes $\{\ldots, p_i, p_j, p_k, \ldots\} = \Pi$ may join the system. Based on different assumptions on the number of processes that can *concurrently* be part of the system, the following infinite arrival models are defined:

1. M^b: The number of processes concurrently inside the system is bounded by a constant b in all runs.

2. M^n: The number of processes concurrently inside the system is bounded in each run, but may be unbounded when we consider the union of all the runs.

3. M: The number of processes that join the system in a single run may grow to infinity as the time passes.

The second attribute [11] looks at relaxing the general assumption of a fully connected communication network as it is usually found in the static system model by considering that at any time each process may only have a partial view of the system. The following *geographical* attributes are defined:

1. At any time, the system can be represented by a graph $G = (P, E)$, where P is the set of processes currently in the system and E is a set of pairs (p_i, p_j) that describe a symmetric neighborhood relation connecting some pairs of processes. $(p_i, p_j) \in E$ means that there is a bidirectional reliable channel connecting p_i and p_j.

2. The dynamicity of the system, i.e., the arrivals and departures of processes, is modeled through additions and removals of vertices and edges in the graph.

   (a) The addition of a process p_i to a graph G brings to another graph G' obtained from G by including p_i and a certain number of new edges $(p_i\ p_j)$ where the p_j are the processes to which p_i is directly connected.

   (b) the removal of a process p_i to a graph G brings to another graph G' obtained from G by suppressing the vertex p_i and all the edges involving p_i.

   (c) Some new edges can be added to the graph, and existing edges can be suppressed from the graph. Each such addition/deletion brings the graph G into another graph G'.

3. Let $\{G_n\}_{run}$ denote the sequence of graphs through which the system passes during a given run. Each $G_n \in \{G_n\}_{run}$ is a *connected graph the diameter of which can be greater than one* for all runs.

   Unless otherwise specified, the *static system model* with a finite set of processes and a fully connected communication graph of reliable point-to-point links is assumed when talking about consensus.

6.2.3 BYZANTINE FAULT TOLERANCE

So far, we have not adequately addressed the question of how consensus protocols can deal with more severe failures than the relatively benign crash-stop model. When the consensus problem was first outlined by Pease, Shostak, and Lamport in [126], no explicit differentiation or limitation of failure models was made, thereby allowing processes to exhibit arbitrary or *Byzantine* failures. The motivation for their work emerged from the development of fault-tolerant systems where consensus, in particular *interactive consistency*, was needed in various aspects of the design, such as synchronization of clocks, stabilization of sensor inputs, and system diagnostics. The realization that simple majority voting schemes would not be sufficient to guarantee consistency if faulty processes could send differing answers to processes led to the question under which conditions such interactive consistency could actually be achieved.

In their subsequent seminal work on the *Byzantine Generals Problem* Lamport, Shostak, and Pease [101] introduced the term *Byzantine general* to describe a faulty node that may act maliciously. Beyond the strong impact this work has had on the research field of fault-tolerant systems, the term *Byzantine* has subsequently been adopted as a descriptor for arbitrary or malicious failures. The ability to withstand such Byzantine failures is referred to as *Byzantine fault tolerance* or BFT. As outlined above, there is generally no distinction between arbitrary and Byzantine failures because a sequence of randomly occurring arbitrary faults may behave in the exact same way as a coordinated malicious entity.

In the following pages we will first outline the concept of *interactive consistency* that was described in [126], before moving on to the more commonly known *Byzantine generals problem*. There has been, and still is, some confusion and uncertainty regarding the terminology used to describe different consensus problems in the Byzantine failure model. In particular the terms *Byzantine agreement* and *Byzantine consensus* do not necessarily refer to the same class of consensus problems. These differences are also addressed when speaking about the Byzantine generals problem.

Interactive Consistency

Interactive consistency is the notion that a set of processes reach agreement upon a vector of values such that each correct process outputs the same vector, and that each element of the vector either corresponds to the private output of a given correct process, or, if the corresponding process is faulty, some other agreed upon value. In [126] interactive consistency was considered in the following context.

A synchronous system consisting of a set of processes $\{p_1, p_2, \ldots, p_n\} = \Pi$ connected through reliable point-to-point links is assumed. Processes are to agree upon the same vector of values $\{v_1, v_2, \ldots, v_n\} = V$ where v_i corresponds to some private value of information of process p_i, and where a maximum of f processes out of n may fail arbitrarily. Analogously to the previously defined consensus problem, we can give the following definition (Definition 6.5) for interactive consistency:

Definition 6.5   The interactive consistency problem defined by three properties:

1. **Validity:** If p_i is a correct process, then element v_i of vector V corresponds to the private value of p_i.

2. **Agreement:** Correct processes agree upon exactly the same vector V.

3. **Termination:** Every correct process (eventually) decides some vector V.

What Pease et. al were able to show in [126] is that in order to be able to guarantee these properties, a total of $n \geq 3f + 1$ processes is required to tolerate f faulty processes in a model that uses so-called *oral messages* for communication. On the other hand, if a stronger primitive called *authenticated messages* is available an *arbitrary*[9] number of failures can be tolerated, i.e., $n \geq f \geq 0$. Authenticated messages basically strengthen the assumptions such that messages from correct processes become tamper-proof and their authorship can be ascertained. As such, Byzantine processes are limited in their available actions and can only choose to withhold or forward messages at a particular time as any modifications to the message would be detectable under the assumed properties. Oral messages have been defined in [101] through the following characteristics:

Definition 6.6   Properties for *oral* messages:

1. Every message that is sent is delivered correctly.

2. The receiver of a message knows who sent it.

3. The absence of a message can be detected.

The second property, in particular, is needed, or else a single (Byzantine) failed process could defeat any distributed algorithm [100]. For the case of authenticated messages,[10] an additional fourth assumption is added to the previous Definition 6.6:

Definition 6.7   Additional fourth property for *authenticated* messages:

4. (a) Messages sent by a correct process cannot be forged, and any alteration of the contents of these signed messages can be detected.

   (b) Anyone can verify the authenticity of a correct process's signature.

It is clear that the addition of message authentication can greatly improve the resilience toward Byzantine failures, at least in *synchronous* system models.

As will be discussed later, in an asynchronous system model, even if message authentication is available the lower bound for failures remains $f < \lceil \frac{n}{3} \rceil$.

Byzantine Agreement and the Byzantine Generals Problem
In the literature, there is often no clear differentiation of the nomenclature for certain different consensus problems in the Byzantine failure model. Byzantine agreement may refer to both the previously described *consensus problem* in the Byzantine failure model and the *Byzantine generals problem*. In the latter case, the goal is to have a distinguished leader send its private value to all processes, after which all correct processes are to either agree upon that value or agree that the sender was faulty. This problem is actually a form of *reliable broadcast*, specifically (terminating)

---

[9]However, the problem becomes vacuous if $n < f + 2$ [101].
[10]In [101], Lamport et al. called them signed *written* messages.

reliable broadcast in the Byzantine failure model. In [71], Fischer outlines how a solution to interactive consistency can be transformed to the Byzantine generals problem and vice versa, and presents an algorithm that transforms Byzantine consensus to the Byzantine generals problem (in a synchronous system model). It is, however, also pointed out that this algorithm requires one additional round of message communication. Furthermore, as later outlined by [39], terminating reliable broadcast and thus both the Byzantine generals problem and interactive consistency require stronger synchrony assumptions than regular consensus, therefore rendering Byzantine consensus a weaker problem than Byzantine agreement.

From here on, the term *Byzantine consensus* will exclusively refer to the consensus problem in a Byzantine failure model, whereas *Byzantine agreement* will be used to refer to the *Byzantine generals problem* or *Byzantine Terminating Reliable Broadcast*. The following definition describes the Byzantine generals problem as presented by Lamport et al. in [99]:

Definition 6.8   The *Byzantine generals problem* or *Byzantine agreement*:
Given a collection of processes numbered from 0 to $n - 1$ which communicate by sending messages to one another, to find an algorithm by which Process 0 can transmit a value v to all processes such that:

1. If Process 0 is nonfaulty, then any nonfaulty Process i obtains the value v.

2. If Process i and j are nonfaulty, then they both obtain the same value.

In [30], Bracha and Toueg show that it is also impossible to guarantee *Byzantine reliable broadcast*,[11] a weaker problem than Byzantine agreement, with $f \geq \lceil \frac{n}{3} \rceil$ in an asynchronous system model with oral messages. In other words, the requirement of $n \geq 3f + 1$ also applies to solutions of asynchronous Byzantine reliable broadcast.

Definition 6.9   Byzantine reliable broadcast:

1. If the transmitter is correct, all the correct processes decide on its value.

2. If the transmitter is malicious, then either no correct process will decide or they will all decide on the same value.

Note that the definition does not include the *termination* property of consensus or TRB and a faulty transmitter can therefore prevent all correct processes from delivering a message. This weakened guarantee is necessary in an asynchronous system or else solutions would have to contradict the FLP impossibility result.

---

[11] In [30] Bracha and Toueg use the term Byzantine agreement to refer to this problem.

Oracles in BFT

Analogous to approaches for consensus in the crash-stop failure model some form of *oracle* may also be employed to augment the system model and render Byzantine consensus or Byzantine agreement solvable in the asynchronous case. The following two approaches, namely *failure detectors* and *wormholes*, both shift the required synchrony assumptions out of the direct scope of the problem by providing an abstraction that protocols can rely on.

Failure Detectors   One might assume that the failure detector abstraction presented by Chandra and Toueg [39] can be directly applied to the Byzantine failure model, but this is not the case. While in the crash-stop model, the behavior of a faulty process is well defined, this is not the case for Byzantine failures where a faulty process may exhibit all sorts of different behaviors or, for some time, even act according to the protocol specification. Doudou et al. [61] outline that the detection of Byzantine behavior of a process p by a Byzantine failure detector cannot be entirely independent of the algorithm $\mathcal{A}$ in which the failure detector is used. Kihlstrom et al. [95] also point out that there is a subset of Byzantine faults that cannot be detected.

In [105], Malkhi and Reiter use an approach where they define a Byzantine failure detector class $\diamond S(bz)$ that only detects (quiet) behaviors that may prevent progress and defers all other forms of Byzantine failure detection to upper levels of the consensus protocol. Such a failure detector that detects if a process stops sending messages has also been defined by Doudou et al. as a so-called *muteness failure detector* [61]. The properties of such a muteness failure detector, denoted by $\diamond M_{\mathcal{A}}$, are:

Definition 6.10   Muteness failure detector

1. **Mute $\mathcal{A}$-Completeness.** There is a time after which every process that is mute to a correct process p, with respect to $\mathcal{A}$, is suspected by p forever.

2. **Eventual Weak $\mathcal{A}$-Accuracy.** There is a time after which a correct process p is no more suspected to be mute, with respect to $\mathcal{A}$, by any other correct process.

Wormholes   Wormholes are closely related to the notion of *architectural hybridization* and encapsulate and provide stronger guarantees to an otherwise weaker environment [48]. The concept of wormholes was introduced in [146] and essentially follows the idea that instead of trying to implement or provide difficult-to-achieve properties in a specific system model, one could create a subsystem where such properties are more readily achieved and allow processes (limited) access to this subsystem.

Instead of presenting an abstraction that specifies the minimum requirements (such as the ability to detect failures), wormholes provide the ability to introduce controllable levels of predictability into systems that are otherwise mostly uncertain with regard to their provided guarantees.

By relying on wormholes, it is possible to further improve upon bounds such as the resilience to failures, which would otherwise not be possible.

Correia et al. [47], for instance, present a method for achieving "asynchronous" Byzantine consensus with $n \geq 2f + 1$ processes by combining a *muteness failure detector* and a reliable broadcast protocol that is augmented through wormholes to tolerate an arbitrary number f of faulty processes. Their approach can be used to transform any *indulgent* consensus algorithm that tolerates crash failures and requires $n \geq 2f + 1$ processes into a similar one that tolerates Byzantine failures and requires $n \geq 2f + 1$ processes. They provide examples for how both a randomized asynchronous algorithm (Ben-Or) and a partially synchronous (asynchronous but augmented with unreliable failure detectors) algorithm (Mostefaoui and Raynal consensus [115]) can be modified using these abstractions.

This result does not contradict the previously established lower bounds for Byzantine consensus in such models, which is $n \geq 3f + 1$, because the system is in fact a *hybrid*, where the stronger (synchronous) system model of the wormholes makes these results possible.[12]

Practical Byzantine Fault Tolerance

The feasibility of implementing Byzantine fault-tolerant consensus protocols and BFT state machine replication was initially largely dismissed as impractical for real-world scenarios. Especially considering the rather limited networking and computation capacities of the time, it would have been difficult to justify the large communication overhead and relatively strong synchrony requirements in non-specialized systems. Instead, focus was largely placed on the crash-fault-tolerant system model.

This is in contrast to statements in some of the early works on Byzantine consensus, especially those considering randomization [45, 130], that already pointed out that the proposed protocols would lend themselves to practical implementations.

In 1999, Castro and Liskov presented a protocol for "Practical Byzantine Fault Tolerance" [36] that illustrated practicability by providing tangible performance metrics, thereby changing the general conception on the real-world feasiblity of BFT. Generally referred to as *PBFT*, their BFT state machine replication protocol is able to operate efficiently even under relatively weak synchrony assumptions. Specifically, the liveness guarantee only holds if at most $f \leq \lfloor \frac{n-1}{3} \rfloor$ replicas are faulty and the *delay(t)*, i.e., the time between the moment t when a message is sent for the first time and the moment when it is received by its destination, does not grow indefinitely. PBFT relies on authenticated messages and on the (asynchronous) network with unreliable links still allowing eventual progress to be made. More recent works on BFT protocols have improved on both the efficiency and performance of PBFT [84, 97], and such systems show that processing tens of thousands of transactions per second is possible with relatively low latency and that they can operate in environments with rather weak synchrony guarantees, such as the Internet or other large-scale WANs. The term *practical Byzantine fault tolerance* itself may

---

[12]In a synchronous system with authenticated messages, Byzantine consensus is possible for $n \geq f \geq 0$.

also be used in other contexts, such as randomized Byzantine consensus algorithms [34], and should not be treated as a synonym for the PBFT protocol or derivatives thereof. Despite the recent improvements in BFT state machine replication and Byzantine consensus protocols in both the deterministic and probabilistic setting, such protocols have yet to see widespread adoption in real-world systems.

6.2.4   RANDOMIZED CONSENSUS PROTOCOLS

An entirely different approach to solving consensus in the asynchronous system model and to dealing with the FLP impossibility result based on *randomization* was pioneered by Ben-Or [16] and Rabin [130] in 1983, thereby creating the field of fault-tolerant randomized distributed algorithms. In 2015, both of these publications were jointly awarded the Edsger W. Dijkstra Prize in Distributed Computing.[13]

For *randomized consensus*, the *termination* property of the *consensus problem* is weakened to:

Definition 6.11   Termination property for *randomized consensus*:

> **Termination with probability 1:** Every correct process eventually decides some value with probability 1.

What this means is that, rather than requiring all permissible executions of a protocol to eventually terminate, executions in the randomized approach may not actually terminate, but this occurs with probability $Pr(0)$ as the number of communication rounds R approaches $\lim_{R \to \infty}$.

Some randomized consensus solutions may also consider a model where the *agreement* property is weakened, so that consensus is always reached within a *finite* number of rounds, albeit only with probability $Pr(1 - \alpha)$, and a probability $Pr(\alpha)$ of error. Such protocols are referred to as *Monte Carlo* randomized consensus algorithms [90]. In [130], for example, Rabin presents a protocol where, for a fixed number of rounds R, the probability of error is $\alpha = Pr(2^{-R})$.

While both Ben-Or and Rabin present solutions to the consensus problem in asynchronous systems that rely on randomization, their approaches differ from one another. Both system models assume a bounded set of $\{p_1, p_2, \ldots, p_n\} = \Pi$ processes, of which at most f may be faulty and where any process p can directly exchange messages with p' that are eventually delivered (asynchronous reliable communication).

Local Coin Randomized Consensus

In Ben-Or's model, processes communicate via *oral messages*.[14] For these oral messages, it is assumed that the receiver p' is always able to determine the true sender p of message m, even in

---

[13]See http://www.podc.org/dijkstra/2015-dijkstra-prize/.
[14]The term *oral message* is defined and explained in 6.2.3 in more detail.

the presence of Byzantine faults. Also, each process $p \in \Pi$ can draw upon a *local coin* that returns, with equal probability $Pr(\frac{1}{2})$, a value $v \in \{0, 1\}$. The solution is given for *binary consensus*, and protocols are presented for both the *crash failure* and the *Byzantine failure model*. In the crash-failure model the total number of processes n must exceed f faulty processes by $n \geq 2f + 1$, and in the Byzantine failure model $n \geq 5f + 1$ is required. This algorithm is actually *optimal* in respect to the maximum number of *crash-failures* it can tolerate, as in such a system model consensus with $n < 2f + 1$ is impossible [29].

The protocols perform rounds of exchange of information where, if a process decides on v in a round r, all correct processes will decide on v by the next round $r + 1$. If no process decides, then with bounded positive probability all correct processes will decide on the next round.

Interestingly, the first *full* correctness proof of Ben-Or's algorithm (for the crash-failure model) was published much later, in 2012 [5].

In this proof it is not only shown that the assumptions hold for $n \geq 2f + 1$ and a *strong adversary*, that is, an adversary that can see process states and message contents as well as schedule process steps and message receipts, but it is also demonstrated that replacing the local coin source of randomness for protocols like that of Ben-Or with a *global coin* in an effort to speed up termination can actually be deleterious and may prevent termination.

Global Coin Randomized Consensus

Another interesting aspect of some randomized consensus protocols is the possibility that consensus can be reached within an *expected* number of communication rounds that is less than $f + 1$, which has been shown to be the lower bound in worst-case executions for a number of deterministic consensus problems, such as Byzantine generals in both the authenticated and unauthenticated case, unauthenticated interactive consistency, and unauthenticated crash-resilient weak consensus [71].

However, Ben-Or's algorithm is not very efficient in this regard, and the expected number of rounds to reach agreement is constant only if $f = O(\sqrt{n})$, otherwise the expected number of rounds may actually be exponential.

The solution presented by Rabin in [130] solves Byzantine consensus[15] within an expected small constant number of rounds independent of n and faulty processes f. The system model assumes reliable communication with *authenticated messages* where processes are supplied in advance with both a directory of public keys and a sequence of random bits as a *shared secret*[16] by a non-faulty dealer. In this case, the shared secret acts as a source of randomness, i.e., a shared *global coin* that allows the protocol to reach agreement in constant expected time as opposed to the exponential time of algorithms as that of Ben-Or. The algorithm requires $n \geq 10f + 1$ for the asynchronous and $n \geq 4f + 1$ for the synchronous case.

---

[15] Note that in [130] Rabin speaks about the Byzantine generals problem; however, in this case no *distinguished leader* is assumed that broadcasts a message, but rather all processes agree on a common value, implying *Byzantine consensus* rather than Byzantine agreement.

[16] Such as by the secret sharing algorithm presented by Shamir in [138].

In [145] Toueg presents a modified version of Rabin's algorithm that solves (Byzantine) randomized consensus for $n \geq 3f + 1$ with an expected number of rounds that is also a small constant independent of n and f but with a higher communication complexity, and also proves that this is the lower bound on the number of failures f for solving asynchronous consensus in the Byzantine failure model, even if authenticated messages are assumed.

Randomization and Byzantine Fault Tolerance

The first randomized consensus algorithms [16, 130] presented their solutions in the context of the Byzantine Generals Problem and, therefore, already considered Byzantine failures; however, their bounds on the number of permissible faulty processes f were not yet optimal. Shortly thereafter it was shown that no Byzantine agreement protocol in an asynchronous system model can achieve resilience against $f \geq \lceil \frac{n}{3} \rceil$ failures [29], even if message authentication is assumed [145]. In other words, the system requires at least $n \geq 3f + 1$ processes, of which at most f can be faulty.

Interestingly, these early works not only considered randomized Byzantine consensus algorithms where the termination property was weakened to *termination with probability* $Pr(1)$, but also variants where correct agreement is only achieved with a certain probability $Pr(1 - \alpha)$, which is dependent on the number of (fixed) rounds the algorithm is executed.

Such randomized consensus with a non-deterministic agreement property has since been largely overlooked as a topic of research [48]. In [90], Ishii and Tempo introduce the terms *Las Vegas* and *Monte Carlo* randomized algorithms to differentiate between consensus that may produce an incorrect result with bounded probability (Monte Carlo) and algorithms that always return the correct answer but where the running time is random.

As we will discuss in 6.3, the guarantees of Nakamoto consensus actually also relate to this non-deterministic agreement property, as consensus on a block in the blockchain is only guaranteed with a certain probability that increases exponentially toward $Pr(1)$ as the protocol progresses.

As we have outlined, randomized consensus protocols exist that are able to reach agreement with probability $Pr(1)$ within a small *constant* expected number of steps independent of n and f. In particular, the *global coin* model that was introduced by Rabin [130] has drawn the attention of further research, as it avoids the problem generally found in *local coin* approaches such as that of Ben-Or, which can have an expected exponential number of rounds if there are many faulty processes. On the other hand, the local coin model's advantages are that algorithms can be much simpler in their implementation and do not have to rely on cryptography. Drawbacks of Rabin's approach were that a *trusted dealer* is required for the initial distribution of the global coin shares and that this shared randomness is eventually consumed. These problems of needing to rely on a trusted dealer for initial shared coin distribution and exhausting the shared coin have been addressed in further work [34, 35].

It has often been assumed that randomized consensus algorithms are impractical due to their high expected message and time complexities [48]. Such assumptions, perhaps, do not consider the often quite strong adversarial model under which these algorithms are considered, which does not reflect practical real-world conditions. Moniz et al. [113], for instance, analyze and compare both local and global coin probabilistic binary Byzantine consensus algorithms in a realistic setup and show that both can be practical. In particular, their results showed that:

1. Shared coin protocols (SCP) are more robust toward malicious faults than local coin-based protocols (LCP), since their performance was not affected when malicious faults were injected.

2. LCP is significantly faster than SCP with similar system parameters for all tested environmental settings.

3. The measured average number of rounds for both protocols was quite small, being close to one with no faults and exactly one with f *crashed* processes. For *Byzantine failures*, SCP scored similar to the failure-free scenario, while LCP showed small degradations that were accentuated with higher n.[17]

4. SCP was slower but proved to be more scalable when the total number of nodes n increases as its performance degraded to a lesser degree than LCP.

5. The bottleneck for LCP was network bandwidth because of the high number of exchanged messages, whereas for SCP it was the CPU because of expensive asymmetric cryptography, suggesting that LCP is more suitable for LAN environments whereas SCP is a better candidate for WAN environments.

In [111] Miller et. al present a practical *asynchronous* BFT protocol whose design is optimized particularly for *cryptocurrency-like deployment scenarios* where bandwidth is the scarce resource that is called *HoneyBadgerBFT*. It extends the work of Cachin et al. [33] on asynchronous (hence randomized) Byzantine fault-tolerant broadcast protocols and improves the previous $O(N^2)$ communication complexity to $O(N)$.

6.3   A CLOSER LOOK AT NAKAMOTO CONSENSUS

So far, this chapter has mainly covered fundamental aspects of consensus and Byzantine fault tolerance without relating them to Bitcoin and Nakamoto consensus. Now that these aspects, and more importantly, the limitations and achievable properties for certain consensus problems have been outlined, we can discuss Nakamoto consensus in this context. Let us first consider some of the unique properties the Bitcoin protocol and its underlying consensus mechanism exhibit.

---

[17]Tests with up to $n = 10$ processes were conducted.

Anonymous Consensus   One of the most interesting aspects of Bitcoin is the ability for anonymous processes to participate in the consensus protocol via proof-of-work mining. A process need not reveal any information about itself prior to disseminating a valid solution to the network. Such a model where "anyone," i.e., *pseudonymous* or *anonymous* entities, can participate in the consensus process and is, in principle, capable of generating new currency units is often referred to as a "permissionless" setting, whereas systems that rely on a trusted set of consensus processes such as designs based on BFT consensus are called "permissioned" [143, 147].

Dynamic Membership with Byzantine Faults   The consensus and BFT protocols so far presented in this publication generally assume a static set of known processes that make up the consensus participants.

Agreeing on a dynamically changing set of processes is, in itself, a problem related to consensus, namely the *Group Membership Problem*. This problem has been studied primarily in the crash-failure model, where the introduction of the concept of *virtual synchrony* by Birman and Joseph [19] in the *ISIS* system has been influential and led to a variety of practical group membership systems such as *JGroups* [13], *Spread* [7], and *Appia* [112].

Byzantine fault tolerance in the context of group membership systems was explored in implementations such as *Rampart* [131] and *SecureRing* [94]; however, in these cases either the problem of dealing with potentially Byzantine processes in the changing membership set is only partially addressed (Rampart), or relatively strong guarantees on aspects such as *synchrony* and the ability to detect Byzantine failures (SecureRing) are assumed.

The difficulties with such systems lie in dealing with Sybil attacks and being able to uphold guarantees if the ratio of honest to faulty processes both within and across *views*[18] changes. In general, Byzantine fault-tolerant dynamic group membership is an ongoing research topic with many open questions that remain to be answered.

The concept of using moderately hard puzzles to expose impostors in Byzantine consensus where processes may assume multiple identities has been outlined by Aspnes et al. in [8]. Bitcoin's proof-of-work follows this mechanism and appears to allow a changing set of processes to form eventual agreement on a blockchain, as long as a sufficiently large majority of active processes is not faulty. As will later be outlined, the specific properties under which Bitcoin and, more generally, Nakamoto consensus can uphold its claimed guarantees is an ongoing field of research.

Consensus Scalability   A problem many classical BFT consensus systems face is the difficulty of efficiently scaling with respect to the number of processes that can actively participate in consensus. The message complexity is usually expected to be quadratic, i.e., $O(n^2)$, and practical systems generally assume a rather small number of processes, ranging from fewer than ten to, at the very most, a few hundred processes.

---

[18]In dynamic group membership, the agreed upon set of processes that constitute the group at a particular time is referred to as a view, and the system progresses through an increasing sequence of views as processes join or leave the agreed upon set.

Beyond the communication overhead for a large set of processes, the focus on small consensus groups may also be attributed to the fact that BFT protocols were often developed in the context of state machine replication in order to provide fault-tolerant replication to some particular service, such as a database, and not as a large decentralized system where a large number of processes may want to participate. Solutions for supporting a larger set of processes in such models may involve the delegation of consensus responsibilities to a select subset of nodes that are responsible for collecting local peer information and including it in their consensus votes as well as disseminating consensus results.

Bitcoin and Nakamoto consensus, on the other hand, can potentially support a very large number of processes that can concurrently participate in consensus because the mining difficulty is adjusted so that on average, a valid solution is found after a certain interval. No communication between nodes is necessary other than the dissemination of newly found blocks. In [147] Vukolić provides a comparison between PBFT and similar permissioned approaches to *permissionless* solutions such as Bitcoin.

6.3.1 DEFINING NAKAMOTO CONSENSUS

There is currently no agreed upon definition of what constitutes Nakamoto consensus, and research on the properties of Bitcoin and other related systems may or may not adhere to this naming convention. Works have also used other names such as *"The Bitcoin Backbone Protocol"* [76] or *"Nakamoto's blockchain protocol"* [123]; however, the term *Nakamoto consensus* is finding its way into more and more publications and we believe it is a suitable descriptor for this novel consensus approach.

It is also possible to define the term *blockchain* in the context of Nakamoto consensus and thereby account for the distributed systems aspects of this technology. This is also done by Pass et al. [123] with their definition of an *abstract blockchain* which is presented in this section (Definition 6.13).

A fundamental difficulty in providing a good generalized definition lies in the tight interaction between the various mechanisms that make up the Bitcoin protocol.

The proof-of-work that is used by nodes to generate new blocks not only provides a form of *probabilistic leader election*, but also serves as a (weak) authentication mechanism that prevents an attacker from carrying out Sybil attacks.

This leader election mechanism is, in fact, a form of consensus that relies upon other nodes to acknowledge the leader, i.e., the creator of a valid block at a particular height, by appending new valid blocks to that block. The depth of a block in a blockchain, or more precisely the cumulative work acknowledging a block by appending to it in relation to the overall computational capacity of the system, gives some outlook on the likelihood that all nodes of the system will agree that this block is part of the blockchain they consider valid.

In [108], Miller and LaViola considered the proof-of-work consensus mechanism of Bitcoin for a single instance, specifically for reaching eventual *binary consensus*, which they simply refer to as a *"Bitcoin Consensus Protocol."* In particular, they relate it to *Monte Carlo* random-ized consensus, that is, probabilistic consensus where there is a non-zero probability of error on agreement.

Monte Carlo Consensus: A Monte Carlo consensus protocol for a set of n processes (f of which may be corrupted) begins with each correct process p_i receiving an input value *proposed$_i$* $\in$ $\{0, 1\}^*$, and must satisfy the following properties:

1. **Termination:** All correct processes must output a single value after a bounded time.

2. **Agreement:** All correct processes must output *the same value*, except with *negligible probability*.

3. **Validity:** The output value must be one of the inputs (*with non-negligible probability*).

Instead of constructing a concatenated blockchain, processes exchange their preferences with proofs-of-work and adopt, as their own preference, the value that appears to have the most votes. Their model assumes a set of processes $\{p_1, p_2, \ldots, p_n\} = \Pi$ where each process p_i starts with a value $v_i \in \{0, 1\}$. Both communication and processing time are assumed to be synchronous and reliable; however, processes have no way of determining message origins. Under these assumptions, Miller and LaViola [108] show that such a *Bitcoin Consensus Protocol* can satisfy the presented Monte Carlo consensus properties for an adversary that controls strictly less than half, i.e., $\sum_{b \in \mathcal{B}(t)} m(b) < 50\%$ of the computing power.

Interestingly, this result regarding failure resilience for single consensus of what we may consider a variant of Nakamoto consensus does not easily translate to consensus for multiple instances, which is required when considering a blockchain data structure or different system states for state machine replication.

In a multiple instance model, adversaries may adopt certain strategies such as block-withholding attacks [69, 120] that are not relevant in the single instance consensus model.

Eyal et al. [68] define Nakamoto consensus in the context of state machine replication. In their model the system is comprised of a set of processes $\{p_1, p_2, \ldots, p_n\} = \Pi$ connected by a reliable peer-to-peer network.

Each process has access to a random bit source through a (cryptographic) *random oracle*. Processes can generate key pairs but no trusted PKI is assumed. A cryptographic proof-of-work scheme as described in Chapter 2 is assumed, where each process $p \in \Pi$ has a limited computation power.

The mining power of process p_i, denoted by $m(i)$, is the number of attempts per second a given process can make when searching for a solution to the PoW with respect to its limited compute power. At any time t a subset of nodes $\mathcal{B}(t) \subset \Pi$ are Byzantine where, based on the previous findings on selfish mining by Eyal and Sirer [69], they assume an upper bound on the combined mining power of $\mathcal{B}(t)$ at any time t that is:

$$\forall t : \sum_{b \in \mathcal{B}(t)} m(b) < \frac{1}{4} \sum_{p \in \Pi} m(p).$$

Or, in other words, the combined mining power of Byzantine nodes at any time is to be less than $\frac{1}{4}$. In their model Nakamoto consensus is expressed through the following three properties:

Definition 6.12   Properties of Nakamoto consensus as by Eyal et al. [68]

1. **Termination:** There exists a time difference function $\Delta(\cdot)$ such that, given a time t and a value $0 < \varepsilon < 1$, the probability is smaller than ε that at times $t', t'' > t + \Delta(\varepsilon)$ a node returns two different states for the machine at time t.

2. **Agreement:** There exists a time difference function $\Delta(\cdot)$ such that, given a $0 < \varepsilon < 1$, the probability that at time t two nodes return different states for $t - \Delta(\varepsilon)$ is smaller than ε.

3. **Validity:** If the fraction of mining power of Byzantine nodes is bounded by f, i.e., $\forall t :$ $\frac{\sum_{b \in \mathcal{B}(t)} m(b)}{\sum_{p \in \Pi} m(p)} < f$, then the average fraction of state machine transitions that are not inputs of honest nodes is smaller than f.

In [76] Garay et al. analyze and formally describe Nakamoto consensus through looking at the "*...core of the Bitcoin protocol,*" and refer to it as the "Bitcoin Backbone Protocol." Its fundamental characteristics are described through two properties, called the *common prefix property* and *chain-quality property*, that are quantified by three parameters, γ, β and m,[19] where γ and β correspond to the collective hashing power per round of honest nodes and the adversary respectively, and where m represents the expected number of PoWs that may be found per round by the participants as a whole. The system model assumes both a static set of nodes and a synchronous communication model. The *common prefix property* guarantees that if, $\gamma > \lambda\beta$ for some $\lambda \in [1, \infty)$ that satisfies $\lambda^2 - m\lambda + 1 \geq 0$, then the local blockchains of honest nodes will possess a large common prefix. What is meant by this is that the probability for two honest nodes to maintain mutual prefixes of their blockchains by removing k blocks from the top of their local chains increases exponentially in k. The *chain-quality property* states that if $\gamma > \lambda\beta$ for some $\lambda \in [1, \infty)$, then the ratio of blocks contributed by honest players in the chain of any honest player is at least $(1 - \frac{1}{\lambda})$.

Another definition by Pass et al. in [123] expresses Nakamoto consensus, or what they refer to as "*the core blockchain protocol,*" as an *abstract blockchain* that should satisfy the following four key properties:

Definition 6.13   *Abstract blockchain*

[19]In [76] Garay et al. use the variable f, however we already employ f to denote the number of faulty processes and hence divert to using m.

1. **T-consistency:** with overwhelming probability (in T), at any point, the chains of two honest players can differ only in the last T blocks.

2. **future self-consistency:** with overwhelming probability (in T), at any two points r, s the chains of any honest player at r and s differ only within the last T blocks.

3. **g-chain-growth:** with overwhelming probability (in T), at any point in the execution, the chain of honest players grows by at least T messages in the last $\frac{T}{g}$ rounds; g is called the chain-growth of the protocol.

4. the μ-**chain quality:** with overwhelming probability (in T), for any T consecutive messages in any chain held by some honest player, the fraction of messages that were "contributed by honest players" is at least μ.

In the same work they analyze Nakamoto consensus based on these properties in an asynchronous system model and show that it can neither satisfy consistency nor chain quality without an upper bound Δ on the network delay, even if the adversary only controls a tiny fraction of computational power.[20] Furthermore, it is shown that, as long as the adversary controls less than half of the computational power ($\rho < \frac{1}{2}$), for every Δ there exists some sufficiently small mining-hardness p (if $p > \frac{1}{\rho n \Delta}$ consistency can't be satisfied) so that Nakamoto consensus satisfies *T-consistency*, thereby extending previous findings by Garay et al. that have shown Nakamoto consensus to satisfy consistency in the synchronous system model [76].

At the time of writing, the properties and characteristics of Bitcoin and Nakamoto consensus are still an ongoing subject of research.

Summary

In this chapter, we have shown that reaching agreement in the presence of faults, i.e., *consensus*, is a non-trivial problem whose solvability greatly depends on the characteristics of the assumed system model. Considering weak models of *synchrony* and the presence of *Byzantine failures* renders the consensus problem harder to the point that early solutions were considered impractical for real-world implementations. Only once broadly available computational and networking resources had increased sufficiently in capacity and Byzantine consensus protocols had been improved did Byzantine fault tolerance become feasible. Byzantine fault tolerant consensus is an essential building block for distributed systems where the amount of trust in participating nodes is to be minimized. The Bitcoin protocol at its core also belongs to the general class of Byzantine consensus protocols. On the one hand, its assumptions render the consensus problem harder by allowing *anonymous participants*, thereby opening the door to Sybil attacks. On the other hand, the agreement property of consensus is weakened to a form of Monte Carlo consensus where

---

[20]Specifically when $\Delta = \frac{1+\delta}{\rho n p}$ for some $\delta > 0$, where $\rho n p$ is the expected number of blocks that an attacker can mine in a round.

agreement may be reached with a high probability that increases exponentially; however, there is a non-zero probability of error.

Nakamoto consensus addresses the problem of Byzantine agreement from a novel angle and was introduced in the form of a practical solution to this long-standing problem in fault-tolerant distributed computing. In this respect, the exact guarantees of Nakamoto consensus are still not entirely clear and this area is an ongoing subject of research. We have outlined that (probabilistic) Byzantine agreement is not possible for $n < 3t + 1$ in an asynchronous system model, even if authenticated messages are available. We have also highlighted that using hybrid system models, i.e., wormholes, can help improve upon this result so that Byzantine agreement can be reached in $n \geq 2f + 1$, and Byzantine TRB with $n \geq f$ [15]; however, these wormholes need to rely on synchrony or else they would form a direct contradiction to the previous proofs.

For Nakamoto consensus it was originally assumed that an honest majority of nodes, i.e., $n \geq 2f + 1$, or more precisely honest nodes controlling the majority of computational power, is required to uphold its guarantees.

The original publication by Satoshi Nakamoto [117] did not include formal specifications of the system model or protocol guarantees and has, therefore, left these questions open for further research. Works such as that of Eyal and Sirer [69] as well as [120] have shown that block-withholding strategies exist that can grant *selfish miners* an unfair advantage over honest miners, thereby increasing the requirements for the number of honest nodes to prevent a so-called 51% attack. Under the assumption of a synchronous system, it has been shown that a simplified form of Nakamoto consensus can achieve $n \geq 2f + 1$ for single-instance consensus; however, Nakamoto consensus in the context of a blockchain or state machine replication, i.e., multiple instance consensus, generally requires $f < \lceil \frac{n}{3} \rceil$ to provide the expected guarantees.[21] It has also been shown that in a model of asynchrony, Nakamoto consensus can only provide its guarantees if certain assumptions on the maximum transmission delay in relation to mining difficulty hold [123].

---

[21]For $f < \lceil \frac{n}{2} \rceil$ an adversary may mine a disproportionately large number of blocks relative to their actual hashrate, however honest miners will from time to time have at least one of their blocks included, allowing the basic functionality of a distributed ledger to remain in principle functional (assuming unlimited space to include transactions) albeit not *fair* to honest participants.

CHAPTER 7

Conclusion and Open Challenges

Bitcoin has demonstrated that decentralized cryptographic currencies are technically feasible today. Since going live in early 2009, the Bitcoin protocol and its broader community have proven that it is possible to operate a decentralized global currency capable of performing asset transactions around the world.

At the same time, not only the underlying protocol itself, but the ecosystem as a whole has demonstrated a surprising amount of resilience against a variety of attacks and malicious actors.

Despite these remarkable achievements, there are also many challenges and issues left to resolve. These challenges, which most cryptographic currencies are facing today, are not solely of a technical nature. The security and properties provided by Bitcoin and its derivatives are a combination of technical aspects such as cryptographic primitives and consensus algorithms as well as incentive engineering that relies on mining rewards, and the trust people place in the cryptocurrency, e.g., that bitcoins have and will retain their value. Therefore, cryptographic currencies can be considered as *sociotechnology*, operating at the intersection of society and technology. Since this book focuses on the technical aspects of cryptographic currency technologies, we primarily outline remaining challenges related to technical and usability aspects. While issues related to sociological, political, legal, and regulatory challenges are also of significant importance for the understanding and further development of cryptographic currency technologies and their ecosystems, they lie outside the scope of this book. In the following, we discuss open challenges in the technical domain.

Scalability Bitcoin-like cryptographic currencies that are based on proof-of-work have certain drawbacks when it comes to scalability. Due to network latencies and structure and the very nature of the computationally expensive proof-of-work, there are certain performance limitations. The Bitcoin network is currently capable of handling about 7 to 10 transactions per second [50, 51, 147]. Compared to traditional payment networks, this is a relatively small number. For example, PayPal is capable of handling a few hundred transactions per second [92] whereas VISA can process up to several thousand transactions per second [50, 92]. It is well known that there are certain trade-offs between the security and performance of PoW-based cryptographic currencies [12, 79, 92, 139]. Optimizing the performance of cryptographic currency technologies, i.e., blockchains, while still being able to provide information and accurate estimates on the security impact of any changes is an ongoing topic of research. Several different approaches have been proposed that aim to minimize intrusive changes to existing protocols, such as *Bitcoin-NG* [68]. Others propose switching to entirely different underlying consensus mechanisms [147, 148]. Hybrid system models [125] that aim to consolidate advantages of both approaches are also being discussed. For a general summary of possible directions see [50].

Resource Consumption   All proof-of-work-based schemes rely on the existence of a limited resource that nodes are required to draw upon if they want to provide the PoW. In Bitcoin, this resource is a combination of energy, hardware, and network capacity. If there were a proof-of-work that did not rely on a limited resource and instead could be claimed in unbounded quantities by anybody, then this automatically would mean that the system would be vulnerable to Sibyl attacks. It is actually the "anonymous" and *permissionless* setting of the Bitcoin protocol that allows mining nodes to not reveal any previous information about themselves when presenting a solution to the required proof-of-work. In a non-anonymous setting where nodes may join or leave the system, the problem remains difficult if we are to maintain the trustless model where nodes may behave maliciously.

The question that arises is whether there are provable secure and yet practical and scalable schemes that allow us to virtualize these required PoW resources and still provide protection against Sibyls in the permissionless model. Such a scheme would mean that instead of being forced to waste physical resources such as energy and computation hardware, one would only need to rely on virtual ones. One of the first approaches toward virtualizing such PoW resources, called *proof-of-stake* (PoS), has been introduced for cryptographic currencies such as *Peercoin* [96]. The general idea behind proof-of-stake is to allow participants to lock up or *stake* part of their cryptocurrency units, which, in relation to the number of units staked by other miners, gives them a certain probability at which they can mine, or *mint*, a new block. Several difficulties and attacks with regard to proof-of-stake cryptocurrencies have been initially pointed out [17], and until recently, concepts and presented protocols often lacked formal models and security proofs. This situation however has been amended by recent works such as those of Kiayias et al. [93] and Bentov et al. [18], which both present provably secure proof-of-stake blockchain protocols. It appears to be that a crucial component for achieving security in such protocols is the existence or joint generation of a sufficiently unbiased random oracle such as a *global random coin*.

Another approach toward improving the security of proof-of-stake protocols that is, for instance, being pursued by the Ethereum Foundation is to integrate or leverage economic incentives in the PoS consensus process. The proposed protocol, named *Slasher* [31], is designed to render (certain types of) malicious behavior detectable and consequently *punish* such behavior by destroying locked up funds or potential block rewards of the perpetrator.

The topic of virtualizing PoW resources is still an ongoing field of research and the impact of newer protocol proposals and concepts is yet to be seen.

Centralization vs. Decentralization   Studies on the mining landscape of Bitcoin as well as on other cryptographic currencies show that there is a trend toward centralization even in decentralized PoW-based systems. The question is, how decentralized should a cryptographic currency ecosystem be, and what methods can be used to enforce certain levels of decentralization? Which single points of failure are acceptable and which are not—for example, powerful exchanges, mining pools, and influential developers?

In the case of cryptographic currencies that are based on Byzantine fault-tolerant systems, the question is how to compose and maintain a set of trusted nodes for consensus and who decides which nodes are allowed to participate. If the set of consensus nodes is small and static, resilience against Byzantine failures is more readily achievable, however the system is strongly centralized. The question of how to achieve Byzantine fault tolerance in a dynamic group membership setting which could potentially allow for more decentralization remains part of ongoing research.

Updatability   In the wake of the latest software flaws and feature updates of different cryptographic currencies the question arises how to handle updates in a distributed system without a trusted third party.

One possible direction is to encode a formal description of the protocol, e.g., the consensus system in use, into the data structure, on which the nodes agree when reaching consensus. This would allow us to devise a scheme for software updates that relies on the same consensus mechanisms as the rest of the system. In such a scenario, the question arises how to give a voice to every user. For example, in Bitcoin, only the miners have a direct and immediate influence on the consensus process. Exchanges, users, merchants, and developers certainly all have an influence on the broader ecosystem, but it is indirect, by means of mechanisms such as providing the miners with economic incentives or rational arguments rather than directly through the actual consensus protocol of the system.

Coin Management and Usability   As discussed in Chapter 5, managing digital currency is still a major challenge for many users. Due to the decentralized nature of Bitcoin-like cryptocurrencies, users are usually responsible for managing their own digital assets. In the event of an incident, users have to restore their keys based on their own backups. This is substantially different from traditional currencies, which rely on centralized entities such as banks and government institutions. Hence, decentralized cryptocurrencies pose significant challenges and responsibilities for their users. The underlying cryptographic fundamentals are often difficult to understand for non-expert users, so that many find it hard to manage their keys and coins and, therefore, try to shift the responsibilities to third parties, such as hosted wallet providers. Compared to traditional banks, these providers are often hard to trace and are not backed by government institutions and/or insurance companies in case of a security breach. It is also often hard to determine whether these centralized entities are trustworthy or not due to a lack of transparency and unclear and insufficient legal and organizational regulations. As presented in Chapter 5, a large proportion of individuals use hosted CMTs, which contradicts Bitcoin's inherent benefit of decentralization. Hence, a major challenge for designers and researchers is to provide users with sufficiently user-friendly key management and backup tools so that they can responsibly manage their bitcoins without relying on a centralized entity. A major problem inherent to most cryptographic user applications is that they force users to deal with public key cryptography. It remains to be shown which mental models users have and to what extent they understand the concept of public key cryptography. Furthermore, the perfect trade-off between transparency and usability remains to be determined. Another human-computer interaction problem of Bitcoin lies in its use of metaphors. As argued in Chapter 5, Bitcoin heavily makes use of metaphors derived from traditional currency. These metaphors, however, are often misleading, hindering users' ability to understand what is happening when interacting with the decentralized currency, e.g., processing a payment.

Recovery   Cryptographic currencies put the responsibility for their digital assets, e.g., bitcoins, in the hands of the user. It is possible for the user to make mistakes or for the security of her system to become compromised. Therefore, technologies and best practices are required that work as safety nets, for example multi-party signatures, hardware wallets, or cold storage. Although technically such methods already exist, most common wallet software does not support these technologies. Moreover, further research is required regarding possible accounting strategies for currency units where the secret key has already been destroyed. In this case, it is important that the immutability and pseudonymity requirements of the underlying blockchain, i.e., the ledger not be violated or weakened. Possibilities like [114] are only the tip of the iceberg.

7.1   CONCLUSION

The Bitcoin protocol is a clever mixture of technologies and concepts from different fields which in combination created something remarkable. Most of the used primitives, like chaining of cryptographic hash functions, asymmetric cryptography, or proof-of-work, were known and had been studied for a while before Bitcoin was conceived. The novelty of Bitcoin lies in the fusion of these building blocks with an incentive system based on game theory and a practical use case, namely a digital currency. This created a new type of probabilistic distributed consensus system dubbed *Nakamoto consensus*. The novelty of this mechanism is that it allows the "anonymous" participation in the consensus process through the process of mining without requiring any kind of trusted setup procedure in advance.

Bitcoin is not the answer to everything, but it has undoubtedly had an impact in a number of different areas and communities:

It created a new class of randomized consensus systems and rekindled research in the field of distributed consensus and Byzantine fault-tolerant systems in general. It bootstrapped a vivid and diverse community that is driving the development of this set of technologies further. The original online publication, software implementation, and further development by the community in its early days outpaced traditional academic research and publishing cycles. It demonstrated that you can implement and run a decentralized digital currency system with a market capitalization in the billions of dollars before even having a sound theoretical model of why it works. It showcased that interdisciplinary thinking can lead to novel approaches and solutions with practical applications.

While Bitcoin and blockchains are hardly the answer to life, the universe and everything, as ideologists or advertising sometimes paint it, the fusion of its underlying technologies and methods has opened new pathways and outlined new possibilities in different areas of research. Furthermore, cryptographic currency technologies also have a sociological and practical dimension with disruptive potential. Never before was it this easy to create a currency that can be used worldwide without the absolute need for a trusted third party or the requirement to distribute physical coins and notes. This change of paradigm forces us to rethink the concept of money and currencies and enables us to envision a future in which a multitude of different cryptographic currencies exist, all of which encode their individual techniques and a set of rules accepted within the community of their users. As long as there are methods to easily use different cryptographic currencies and also exchange assets between them, it is not necessary to rely on just one cryptocurrency for everything.

APPENDIX A

Glossary

Cryptographic currencies are a relatively new field of research, hence the nomenclature has not settled for certain terms and their interpretation. Also the spelling is not always universally agreed upon, for example in the case of *blockchain* or *block chain*.[1] This chapter aims to provide rich a glossary of important terms and phrases used throughout the book to avoid ambiguities.

---

[1] Both forms have been used on various occasions but lately the variant without space is becoming predominant. This is also the reason why we adhere to term *blockchain* within this work.

Glossary

blockchain or block chain

There are multiple definitions of the term *blockchain* of which we present two different categories in this book. The broad *Princeton definition* describes a blockchain as a linked list data structure that uses hash sums over its elements as pointers to the respective elements. See Definition 4.1 for details. In Section 6.3 various definitions are presented that place a stronger focus on the formalization of the Bitcoin protocol and its governing mechanisms and which consider the concept of a blockchain from a more abstract vantage point.
Pages: 3, 22

permissioned-, consortium-, private-, or BFT blockchain

The central property of this type of blockchain is that the set of nodes, amongst which consensus over the state of the chain should be reached, is known and an admission to the consensus set is restricted. Vukolic et al. refers to this type as Byzantine Fault Tolerant (BFT) blockchains [147]. Further distinction can be made between *permissioned* blockchains and *private* blockchain regarding the composition and selection of the set of nodes. [2]
Page: 4

permissionless-, public-, or PoW blockchain

The central property of this type of blockchain is that the identity of nodes, amongst which consensus over the state of the chain should be reached, is either pseudonymous or anonymous and the ability for new nodes to start participating in the consensus protocol is relatively unrestricted. Vukolic et al. refers to this type as proof-of-work (POW) blockchains [147].
Page: 4

cryptocurrency or cryptographic currency

A *cryptographic currency* or *cryptocurrency* is a digital asset system designed to work as a medium of exchange that uses cryptographic primitives to secure the control and creation of currency units.
Page: 3

[2]https://blog.ethereum.org/2015/08/07/on-public-and-private-blockchains/

cryptographic currency-, distributed ledger-, or blockchain technologies

We define the terms *cryptographic currency technologies*, *distributed ledger technologies*, *consensus ledger technologies*, as well as *blockchain technologies* as umbrella terms that refer to the whole set of technologies and techniques that are used within the space of cryptographic currencies, blockchains of different sorts, as well as transaction ledgers, e.g., cryptographic primitives, fault-tolerant distributed computing aspects, game theoretic approaches, networking aspects, language security aspects, etc.
Page: 3

difficulty

The difficulty D is a different way to describe the hardness of the proof-of-work. It is defined as the ratio between the maximum target and the current target:

$$D = \frac{T_{\max}}{T_c}$$

Page: 35

distributed currency

A *distributed cryptographic currency* or *distributed cryptocurrency* is a digital asset system designed to work as a medium of exchange that uses cryptographic primitives to secure the decentralized control and creation of currency units.
Page: 3

Nakamoto consensus

We consider the term *Nakamoto consensus* to refer to the underlying consensus mechanism behind Bitcoin, that allows a dynamic set of anonymous participants in a distributed system to reach eventual agreement[3] by leveraging on the properties of proof-of-work as well as economic incentives.
Page: 3

proof-of-work (PoW)

Represents a system that fullfills the following high-level characteristics (in accordance to [119]):

- The PoW is easy to verify
- The difficulty to compute a PoW is adjustable

---

[3]Eventual agreement in Bitcoin is reached on the transaction set and its ordering within a distributed ledger, however Nakamoto consensus may also be used to agree upon other items.

- The PoW is progress-free, i.e., every participant has a probability to find a valid PoW that is proportianal to his share of invested resources.

Pages: 3, 19

target

The target T describes the validity requirements of a proof-of-work, i.e., the hardness. In Bitcoin a valid PoW is defined as:

$$SHA256^2(\text{block header}) \leq T$$

Page: 34

trusted third party (TTP)

A trusted third party (TTP) refers to the requirement of having an intermediary C between two parties A and B which is required to be trusted so that A and B can transact or interact securely according to the respective protocol.
Page: 3

virtual currency

The European Central Bank redefined the term in 2014 as "a digital representation of value that is neither issued by a central bank or a public authority, nor necessarily attached to a fiat currency, but is accepted by natural or legal persons as a means of payment and can be transferred, stored or traded electronically" [9].
Page: 15

zero bits

Number of leading zero bits of the target T.
Page: 34

Bibliography

[1] Coinmarketcap. http://coinmarketcap.com/

[2] Namecoin. https://namecoin.org/

[3] Requiem of a Bright Idea. http://www.forbes.com/forbes/1999/1101/6411390a.html

[4] H. Abelson, R. Anderson, S. M. Bellovin, J. Benaloh, M. Blaze, W. Diffie, J. Gilmore, P. G. Neumann, R. L. Rivest, J. I. Schiller, et al. The risks of key recovery, key escrow, and trusted third-party encryption. *World Wide Web Journal*, 2(3):241–257, 1997.

[5] M. K. Aguilera and S. Toueg. *The correctness proof of ben-or's randomized consensus algorithm.* Volume 25, pages 371–381. Springer, 2012. DOI: 10.1007/s00446-012-0162-z.

[6] P. C. v. O. Alfred J. Menezes and S. A. Vanstone. *Handbook of Applied Cryptography*, 5th ed. CRC Press, 2001. DOI: 10.1201/9781439821916.

[7] Y. Amir and J. Stanton. The spread wide area group communication system. *Technical Report, TR CNDS-98-4, the Center for Networking and Distributed Systems*, Johns Hopkins University, 1998.

[8] J. Aspnes, C. Jackson, and A. Krishnamurthy. Exposing computationally-challenged byzantine impostors. Department of Computer Science, Technical Report, Yale University, New Haven, CT, 2005.

[9] E. B. Authority. Eba opinion on virtual currencies. http://www.eba.europa.eu/documents/10180/657547/EBA-Op-2014-08+Opinion+on+Virtual+Currencies.pdf, 2014.

[10] A. Back et al. Hashcash-a denial of service counter-measure. http://www.hashcash.org/papers/hashcash.pdf, 2002.

[11] R. Baldoni, M. Bertier, M. Raynal, and S. Tucci-Piergiovanni. Looking for a definition of dynamic distributed systems. In *International Conference on Parallel Computing Technologies*, pages 1–14. Springer, 2007. DOI: 10.1007/978-3-540-73940-1_1.

[12] T. Bamert, C. Decker, L. Elsen, R. Wattenhofer, and S. Welten. Have a snack, pay with bitcoins. In *Peer-to-Peer Computing (P2P), 13th International Conference on*, pages 1–5. IEEE, 2013. DOI: 10.1109/p2p.2013.6688717.

[13] B. Ban. Design and implementation of a reliable group communication toolkit for java. Cornell University, 1998.

[14] G. Becker. Merkle signature schemes, merkle trees and their cryptanalysis. Ruhr-University Bochum, Technical Report, 2008.

[15] Z. Beerliová-Trubíniová, M. Hirt, and M. Riser. Efficient byzantine agreement with faulty minority. In *Proc. of the Advances in Crypotology 13th International Conference on Theory and Application of Cryptology and Information Security*, pages 393–409. Springer-Verlag, 2007. DOI: 10.1007/978-3-540-76900-2_24.

[16] M. Ben-Or. Another advantage of free choice (extended abstract): Completely asynchronous agreement protocols. In *Proc. of the 2nd Annual Symposium on Principles of Distributed Computing*, pages 27–30. ACM, 1983. DOI: 10.1145/800221.806707.

[17] I. Bentov, C. Lee, A. Mizrahi, and M. Rosenfeld. Proof of activity: Extending bitcoin's proof of work via proof of stake [extended abstract] y. *ACM SIGMETRICS Performance Evaluation Review*, 42(3):34–37, 2014. DOI: 10.1145/2695533.2695545.

[18] I. Bentov, R. Pass, and E. Shi. Snow white: Provably secure proofs of stake. `https://eprint.iacr.org/2016/919.pdf`, 2016.

[19] K. Birman and T. Joseph. Exploiting virtual synchrony in distributed systems. *ACM*, Volume 21, 1987. DOI: 10.1145/37499.37515.

[20] A. Biryukov, D. Khovratovich, and I. Pustogarov. Deanonymisation of clients in bitcoin p2p network. In *Proc. of the SIGSAC Conference on Computer and Communications Security*, pages 15–29. ACM, 2014. DOI: 10.1145/2660267.2660379.

[21] A. Biryukov and I. Pustogarov. Bitcoin over tor isn't a good idea. In *Security and Privacy (SP), Symposium on*, pages 122–134. IEEE, 2015. DOI: 10.1109/sp.2015.15.

[22] Bitcoin community. Bitcoin-core source code. `https://github.com/bitcoin/bitcoin`

[23] Bitcoin community. Bitcoin developer guide. `https://bitcoin.org/en/developer-documentation`

[24] Bitcoin community. Bitcoin improvement proposals (bips). `https://github.com/bitcoin/bips`

[25] M. Blaze. Protocol failure in the escrowed encryption standard. In *Proc. of the 2nd Conference on Computer and Communications Security*, pages 59–67. ACM, 1994. DOI: 10.1145/191177.191193.

[26] D. Boneh and V. Shoup. A graduate course in applied cryptography. `https://crypto.stanford.edu/~dabo/cryptobook/`, 2008.

[27] J. Bonneau, A. Miller, J. Clark, A. Narayanan, J. A. Kroll, and E. W. Felten. Sok: Research perspectives and challenges for bitcoin and cryptocurrencies. In *IEEE Symposium on Security and Privacy*, 2015. DOI: 10.1109/sp.2015.14.

[28] J. W. Bos, J. A. Halderman, N. Heninger, J. Moore, M. Naehrig, and E. Wustrow. Elliptic curve cryptography in practice. In *Financial Cryptography and Data Security*, pages 157–175. Springer, 2014. DOI: 10.1007/978-3-662-45472-5_11.

[29] G. Bracha and S. Toueg. Resilient consensus protocols. In *Proc. of the 2nd Annual Symposium on Principles of Distributed Computing*, pages 12–26. ACM, 1983. DOI: 10.1145/800221.806706.

[30] G. Bracha and S. Toueg. Asynchronous consensus and broadcast protocols. Volume 32, pages 824–840. Citeseer, 1985. DOI: 10.1145/4221.214134.

[31] V. Buterin. Slasher: A punitive proof-of-stake algorithm. `https://blog.ethereum.org/2014/01/15/slasher-a-punitive-proof-of-stake-algorithm/`, 2014.

[32] V. Buterin. Chain interoperability. `https://static1.squarespace.com/static/55f73743e4b051cfcc0b02cf/t/5886800ecd0f68de303349b1/1485209617040/Chain+Interoperability.pdfi`, 2016.

[33] C. Cachin, K. Kursawe, F. Petzold, and V. Shoup. Secure and efficient asynchronous broadcast protocols. In *Annual International Cryptology Conference*, pages 524–541. Springer, 2001. DOI: 10.1007/3-540-44647-8_31.

[34] C. Cachin, K. Kursawe, and V. Shoup. Random oracles in constantinople: Practical asynchronous byzantine agreement using cryptography. In *Proc. of the 19th Annual Symposium on Principles of Distributed Computing*, pages 123–132. ACM, 2000. DOI: 10.1145/343477.343531.

[35] R. Canetti and T. Rabin. Fast asynchronous byzantine agreement with optimal resilience. In *Proc. of the 25th Annual Symposium on Theory of Computing*, pages 42–51. ACM, 1993. DOI: 10.1145/167088.167105.

[36] M. Castro, B. Liskov, et al. Practical byzantine fault tolerance. In *OSDI*, Volume 99, pages 173–186, 1999.

[37] Certicom Research. SEC 1: Elliptic Curve Cryptography, Version 2.0. `http://www.secg.org/sec1-v2.pdf`, 2009.

[38] Certicom Research. SEC 2: Recommended elliptic curve domain parameters, version 2.0. `http://www.secg.org/collateral/sec2_final.pdf`, 2010.

[39] T. D. Chandra and S. Toueg. Unreliable failure detectors for reliable distributed systems. Volume 43, pages 225–267. ACM, 1996. DOI: 10.1145/226643.226647.

[40] B. Charron-Bost and A. Schiper. Uniform consensus is harder than consensus, 2004. DOI: 10.1016/j.jalgor.2003.11.001.

[41] D. Chaum. Blind signatures for untraceable payments. In *Advances in Cryptology*, pages 199–203. Springer, 1983. DOI: 10.1007/978-1-4757-0602-4_18.

[42] D. Chaum. Security without identification: Transaction systems to make big brother obsolete. Volume 28, pages 1030–1044. ACM, 1985. DOI: 10.1145/4372.4373.

[43] D. Chaum, A. Fiat, and M. Naor. Untraceable electronic cash. In *Proc. on Advances in Cryptology*, pages 319–327. Springer-Verlag, New York, 1990. DOI: 10.1007/0-387-34799-2_25.

[44] L. Chen, P. Morrissey, N. P. Smart, and B. Warinschi. Security notions and generic constructions for client puzzles. In *International Conference on the Theory and Application of Cryptology and Information Security*, pages 505–523. Springer, 2009. DOI: 10.1007/978-3-642-10366-7_30.

[45] B. Chor and B. A. Coan. A simple and efficient randomized byzantine agreement algorithm. Number 6, pages 531–539. IEEE, 1985. DOI: 10.1109/tse.1985.232245.

[46] H. Cohen, G. Frey, R. Avanzi, C. Doche, T. Lange, K. Nguyen, and F. Vercauteren. *Handbook of Elliptic and Hyperelliptic Curve Cryptography*. CRC Press, 2005. DOI: 10.1201/9781420034981.

[47] M. Correia, G. S. Veronese, and L. C. Lung. Asynchronous byzantine consensus with 2f+ 1 processes. In *Proc. of the Symposium on Applied Computing*, pages 475–480. ACM, 2010. DOI: 10.1145/1774088.1774187.

[48] M. Correia, G. S. Veronese, N. F. Neves, and P. Verissimo. Byzantine consensus in asynchronous message-passing systems: A survey. Volume 2, pages 141–161. Inderscience Publishers, 2011. DOI: 10.1504/ijccbs.2011.041257.

[49] F. Cristian. Understanding fault-tolerant distributed systems. Volume 34, pages 56–78. ACM, 1991. DOI: 10.1145/102792.102801.

[50] K. Croman, C. Decker, I. Eyal, A. E. Gencer, A. Juels, A. Kosba, A. Miller, P. Saxena, E. Shi, and E. Gün. On scaling decentralized blockchains. In *3rd Workshop on Bitcoin and Blockchain Research, Financial Cryptography 16*, 2016. DOI: 10.1007/978-3-662-53357-4_8.

[51] C. Decker and R. Wattenhofer. Information propagation in the bitcoin network. In *Peer-to-Peer Computing (P2P), 13th International Conference on*, pages 1–10. IEEE, 2013. DOI: 10.1109/p2p.2013.6688704.

[52] X. Défago, A. Schiper, and P. Urbán. Total order broadcast and multicast algorithms: Taxonomy and survey. *ACM Computing Surveys (CSUR)*, 36(4):372–421, 2004. DOI: 10.1145/1041680.1041682.

[53] W. Dei. B-money. http://www.weidai.com/bmoney.txt

[54] C. Delporte-Gallet, S. Devismes, H. Fauconnier, F. Petit, and S. Toueg. With finite memory consensus is easier than reliable broadcast. In *International Conference on Principles of Distributed Systems*, pages 41–57. Springer, 2008. DOI: 10.1007/978-3-540-92221-6_5.

[55] T. Dierks and E. Rescorla. The transport layer security (TLS) protocol, version 1.2. RFC 5246 (proposed standard), 2008. Updated by RFCs 5746, 5878, 6176, 7465, 7507, 7568, 7627, 7685. DOI: 10.17487/rfc5246.

[56] Dogecoin community. Dogecoin reference implementation. github.com/dogecoin/dogecoin

[57] D. Dolev. Unanimity in an unknown and unreliable environment. In *Foundations of Computer Science, 22nd Annual Symposium on, (SFCS'81)*, pages 159–168. IEEE, 1981. DOI: 10.1109/sfcs.1981.53.

[58] D. Dolev, C. Dwork, and L. Stockmeyer. On the minimal synchronism needed for distributed consensus. Volume 34, pages 77–97. ACM, 1987. DOI: 10.1145/7531.7533.

[59] D. Dolev, M. J. Fischer, R. Fowler, N. A. Lynch, and H. R. Strong. An efficient algorithm for byzantine agreement without authentication. Volume 52, pages 257–274, 1982. DOI: 10.1016/s0019-9958(82)90776-8.

[60] J. R. Douceur. The sybil attack. In *International Workshop on Peer-to-peer Systems*, pages 251–260. Springer, 2002. DOI: 10.1007/3-540-45748-8_24.

[61] A. Doudou, B. Garbinato, and R. Guerraoui. Encapsulating failure detection: From crash to byzantine failures. In *International Conference on Reliable Software Technologies*, pages 24–50. Springer, 2002. DOI: 10.1007/3-540-48046-3_3.

[62] C. Dwork, N. Lynch, and L. Stockmeyer. Consensus in the presence of partial synchrony. Volume 35, pages 288–323. ACM, 1988. DOI: 10.1145/42282.42283.

[63] C. Dwork and M. Naor. Pricing via processing or combatting junk mail. In *Annual International Cryptology Conference*, pages 139–147. Springer, 1992. DOI: 10.1007/3-540-48071-4_10.

[64] Z. electric coin company. Zcash homepage. `https://z.cash/`

[65] S. Eskandari, D. Barrera, E. Stobert, and J. Clark. A first look at the usability of bitcoin key management. In *Workshop on Usable Security (USEC)*, 2015. DOI: 10.14722/usec.2015.23015.

[66] Ethereum community. Ethereum: A secure decentralised generalised transaction ledger. `https://github.com/ethereum/yellowpaper`

[67] I. Eyal. The miner's dilemma. In *Security and Privacy (SP), Symposium on*, pages 89–103. IEEE, 2015. DOI: 10.1109/sp.2015.13.

[68] I. Eyal, A. E. Gencer, E. G. Sirer, and R. van Renesse. Bitcoin-ng: A scalable blockchain protocol. In *13th USENIX Security Symposium on Networked Systems Design and Implementation (NSDI'16)*. USENIX Association, 2016.

[69] I. Eyal and E. G. Sirer. Majority is not enough: Bitcoin mining is vulnerable. In *Financial Cryptography and Data Security*, pages 436–454. Springer, 2014. DOI: 10.1007/978-3-662-45472-5_28.

[70] H. Finney. Reusable proofs of work (RPOW). `http://web.archive.org/web/20071222072154/http://rpow.net/`, 2004.

[71] M. J. Fischer. The consensus problem in unreliable distributed systems (a brief survey). In *International Conference on Fundamentals of Computation Theory*, pages 127–140. Springer, 1983. DOI: 10.1007/3-540-12689-9_99.

[72] M. J. Fischer and N. A. Lynch. A lower bound for the time to assure interactive consistency. Volume 14, 1982. DOI: 10.1016/0020-0190(82)90033-3.

[73] M. J. Fischer, N. A. Lynch, and M. S. Paterson. Impossibility of distributed consensus with one faulty process. Volume 32, pages 374–382. ACM, 1985. DOI: 10.1145/3149.214121.

[74] Y. Frankel and M. Yung. Escrow encryption systems visited: Attacks, analysis and designs. In *Annual International Cryptology Conference*, pages 222–235. Springer, 1995. DOI: 10.1007/3-540-44750-4_18.

[75] R. Fuzzati. A formal approach to fault tolerant distributed consensus. Ph.D. thesis, EPFL, 2008.

[76] J. Garay, A. Kiayias, and N. Leonardos. The bitcoin backbone protocol: Analysis and applications. In *Advances in Cryptology-EUROCRYPT*, pages 281–310. Springer, 2015. DOI: 10.1007/978-3-662-46803-6_10.

[77] J. A. Garay, A. Kiayias, and N. Leonardos. The bitcoin backbone protocol with chains of variable difficulty. http://eprint.iacr.org/2016/1048.pdf, 2016.

[78] F. C. Gärtner. Fundamentals of fault-tolerant distributed computing in asynchronous environments. *ACM Computing Surveys (CSUR)*, 31(1):1–26, 1999. DOI: 10.1145/311531.311532.

[79] A. Gervais, G. O. Karame, K. Wüst, V. Glykantzis, H. Ritzdorf, and S. Capkun. On the security and performance of proof of work blockchains. https://eprint.iacr.or g/2016/555.pdf, 2016. DOI: 10.1145/2976749.2978341.

[80] A. Gervais, H. Ritzdorf, G. O. Karame, and S. Capkun. Tampering with the delivery of blocks and transactions in bitcoin. In *Proc. of the 22nd Conference on Computer and Communications Security (SIGSAC)*, pages 692–705. ACM, 2015. DOI: 10.1145/2810103.2813655.

[81] I. Giechaskiel, C. Cremers, and K. B. Rasmussen. On bitcoin security in the presence of broken cryptographic primitives. In *European Symposium on Research in Computer Security (ESORICS)*, 2016. DOI: 10.1007/978-3-319-45741-3_11.

[82] J. Göbel, P. Keeler, A. E. Krzesinski, and P. G. Taylor. Bitcoin blockchain dynamics: The selfish-mine strategy in the presence of propagation delay. http://arxiv.org/pd f/1505.05343.pdf, 2015. DOI: 10.1016/j.peva.2016.07.001.

[83] B. Groza and B. Warinschi. Cryptographic puzzles and dos resilience, revisited. *Designs, Codes and Cryptography*, 73(1):177–207, 2014. DOI: 10.1007/s10623-013-9816-5.

[84] R. Guerraoui, N. Knežević, V. Quéma, and M. Vukolić. The next 700 BFT protocols. In *Proc. of the 5th European conference on Computer systems*, pages 363–376. ACM, 2010. DOI: 10.1145/1755913.1755950.

[85] V. Hadzilacos and S. Toueg. A modular approach to fault-tolerant broadcasts and related problems. Technical Report 94-1425, Cornell University, 1994.

[86] D. Hankerson, A. J. Menezes, and S. Vanstone. *Guide to Elliptic Curve Cryptography*. Springer Science and Business Media, 2006. DOI: 10.1007/b97644.

[87] E. Heilman, A. Kendler, A. Zohar, and S. Goldberg. Eclipse attacks on bitcoin's peer-to-peer network. In *24th Security Symposium (USENIX Security 15)*, pages 129–144, 2015.

[88] M. Herlihy. Wait-free synchronization. Volume 13, pages 124–149. ACM, 1991. DOI: 10.1145/114005.102808.

[89] J. Hoffstein, J. Pipher, J. H. Silverman, and J. H. Silverman. *An Introduction to Mathematical Cryptography*, Volume 1. Springer, 2008. DOI: 10.1007/978-1-4939-1711-2.

[90] H. Ishii and R. Tempo. Las vegas randomized algorithms in distributed consensus problems. In *American Control Conference*, pages 2579–2584. IEEE, 2008. DOI: 10.1109/acc.2008.4586880.

[91] J. Katz and Y. Lindell. *Introduction to Modern Cryptography*. CRC Press, 2014.

[92] A. Kiayias and G. Panagiotakos. Speed-security tradeoffs in blockchain protocols. `http s://eprint.iacr.org/2015/1019.pdf`, 2015.

[93] A. Kiayias, A. Russell, B. David, and R. Oliynykov. Ouroboros: A provably secure proof-of-stake blockchain protocol. `https://pdfs.semanticscholar.org/1c14/549f7b a7d6a000d79a7d12255eb11113e6fa.pdf`, 2016.

[94] K. P. Kihlstrom, L. E. Moser, and P. M. Melliar-Smith. The securering group communication system. *ACM Transactions on Information and System Security (TISSEC)*, 4(4):371–406, 2001. DOI: 10.1145/503339.503341.

[95] K. P. Kihlstrom, L. E. Moser, and P. M. Melliar-Smith. Byzantine fault detectors for solving consensus. *The Computer Journal*, Volume 46, pages 16–35. Br Computer Soc., 2003. DOI: 10.1093/comjnl/46.1.16.

[96] S. King and S. Nadal. Ppcoin: Peer-to-peer crypto-currency with proof-of-stake. `https://peercoin.net/assets/paper/peercoin-paper.pdf`, 2012.

[97] R. Kotla, L. Alvisi, M. Dahlin, A. Clement, and E. Wong. Zyzzyva: Speculative byzantine fault tolerance. In *Operating Systems Review (SIGOPS)*, Volume 41, pages 45–58. ACM, 2007. DOI: 10.1145/1323293.1294267.

[98] K. Krombholz, A. Judmayer, M. Gusenbauer, and E. Weippl. The other side of the coin: User experiences with bitcoin security and privacy. In *International Conference on Financial Cryptography and Data Security (FC)*, 2, 2016.

[99] L. Lamport. The weak byzantine generals problem. Volume 30, pages 668–676. ACM, 1983. DOI: 10.1145/2402.322398.

[100] L. Lamport. Using time instead of timeout for fault-tolerant distributed systems. Volume 6, pages 254–280. ACM, 1984. DOI: 10.1145/2993.2994.

[101] L. Lamport, R. Shostak, and M. Pease. The byzantine generals problem. Volume 4, pages 382–401. ACM, 1982. DOI: 10.1145/357172.357176.

[102] Y. Lewenberg, Y. Bachrach, Y. Sompolinsky, A. Zohar, and J. S. Rosenschein. Bitcoin mining pools: A cooperative game theoretic analysis. In *Proc. of the International Conference on Autonomous Agents and Multiagent Systems*, pages 919–927. International Foundation for Autonomous Agents and Multiagent Systems, 2015.

[103] E. Lombrozo, J. Lau, and P. Wuille. Bitcoin improvement proposal 141 (bip141): Segregated witness (consensus layer). https://github.com/bitcoin/bips/blob/master/bip-0141.mediawiki

[104] L. Luu, J. Teutsch, R. Kulkarni, and P. Saxena. Demystifying incentives in the consensus computer. In *Proc. of the 22nd Conference on Computer and Communications Security (SIGSAC)*, pages 706–719. ACM, 2015. DOI: 10.1145/2810103.2813659.

[105] D. Malkhi and M. Reiter. Unreliable intrusion detection in distributed computations. In *Proc. of the 10th Computer Security Foundations Workshop*, pages 116–124. IEEE, 1997. DOI: 10.1109/csfw.1997.596799.

[106] A. J. Menezes, P. C. Van Oorschot, and S. A. Vanstone. *Handbook of Applied Cryptography*. CRC Press, 1996. DOI: 10.1201/9781439821916.

[107] R. C. Merkle. A digital signature based on a conventional encryption function. In *Conference on the Theory and Application of Cryptographic Techniques*, pages 369–378. Springer, 1987. DOI: 10.1007/3-540-48184-2_32.

[108] A. Miller and L. JJ. Anonymous byzantine consensus from moderately-hard puzzles: A model for bitcoin. https://socrates1024.s3.amazonaws.com/consensus.pdf, 2014.

[109] A. Miller, A. Kosba, J. Katz, and E. Shi. Nonoutsourceable scratch-off puzzles to discourage bitcoin mining coalitions. In *Proc. of the 22nd Conference on Computer and Communications Security (SIGSAC)*, pages 680–691. ACM, 2015. DOI: 10.1145/2810103.2813621.

[110] A. Miller, J. Litton, A. Pachulski, N. Gupta, D. Levin, N. Spring, and B. Bhattacharjee. Discovering bitcoin's public topology and influential nodes. http://cs.umd.edu/projects/coinscope/coinscope.pdf, 2015.

[111] A. Miller, Y. Xia, K. Croman, E. Shi, and D. Song. The honey badger of BFT protocols. https://eprint.iacr.org/2016/199.pdf, 2016.

[112] H. Miranda, A. Pinto, and L. Rodrigues. Appia, a flexible protocol kernel supporting multiple coordinated channels. In *Distributed Computing Systems, 21st International Conference on*, pages 707–710. IEEE, 2001. DOI: 10.1109/icdsc.2001.919005.

[113] H. Moniz, N. F. Neves, M. Correia, and P. Verissimo. Experimental comparison of local and shared coin randomized consensus protocols. In *25th Symposium on Reliable Distributed Systems (SRDS'06)*, pages 235–244. IEEE, 2006. DOI: 10.1109/srds.2006.19.

[114] M. Möser, I. Eyal, and E. G. Sirer. Bitcoin covenants. In *Proc. of the 20th International Conference on Financial Cryptography (FC'16)*, 2016. DOI: 10.1007/978-3-662-53357-4_9.

[115] A. Mostéfaoui and M. Raynal. Solving consensus using chandra-toueg's unreliable failure detectors: A general quorum-based approach. In *International Symposium on Distributed Computing*, pages 49–63. Springer, 1999. DOI: 10.1007/3-540-48169-9_4.

[116] A. Mostefaoui, M. Raynal, and F. Tronel. From binary consensus to multivalued consensus in asynchronous message-passing systems. *Information Processing Letters*, 73(5-6):207–212, 2000. DOI: 10.1016/s0020-0190(00)00027-2.

[117] S. Nakamoto. Bitcoin: A peer-to-peer electronic cash system. `https://bitcoin.org/bitcoin.pdf`, 2008.

[118] Namecoin community. Bitcoin wiki—merged mining. `https://en.bitcoin.it/wiki/Merged_mining_specification`

[119] A. Narayanan, J. Bonneau, E. Felten, A. Miller, and S. Goldfeder. Bitcoin and cryptocurrency technologies. `https://d28rh4a8wq0iu5.cloudfront.net/bitcointech/readings/princeton_bitcoin_book.pdf?a=1`, 2016.

[120] K. Nayak, S. Kumar, A. Miller, and E. Shi. Stubborn mining: Generalizing selfish mining and combining with an eclipse attack. In *1st European Symposium on Security and Privacy*, IEEE, 2016. DOI: 10.1109/eurosp.2016.32.

[121] NIST. FIPS 180-4: Secure hash standard (SHS), 2012.

[122] K. Okupski. Bitcoin protocol specification. `https://github.com/minium/Bitcoin-Spec`

[123] R. Pass, L. Seeman, and A. Shelat. Analysis of the blockchain protocol in asynchronous networks. `http://eprint.iacr.org/2016/454.pdf`, 2016. DOI: 10.1007/978-3-319-56614-6_22.

[124] R. Pass and E. Shi. Fruitchains: A fair blockchain. `http://eprint.iacr.org/2016/916.pdf`, 2016.

[125] R. Pass and E. Shi. Hybrid consensus: Scalable permissionless consensus. `https://eprint.iacr.org/2016/917.pdf`, 2016.

[126] M. Pease, R. Shostak, and L. Lamport. Reaching agreement in the presence of faults. Volume 27, pages 228–234. ACM, 1980. DOI: 10.1145/322186.322188.

[127] C. Percival. Stronger key derivation via sequential memory-hard functions. `http://www.bsdcan.org/2009/schedule/attachments/87_scrypt.pdf`, 2009.

[128] D. Project. Dogecoin homepage. `https://dogecoin.com/`

[129] L. Project. Litecoin. `https://litecoin.org/`

[130] M. O. Rabin. Randomized byzantine generals. In *Foundations of Computer Science, 24th Annual Symposium on*, pages 403–409. IEEE, 1983. DOI: 10.1109/sfcs.1983.48.

[131] M. K. Reiter. A secure group membership protocol. Volume 22, page 31, 1996. DOI: 10.1109/32.481515.

[132] A. M. Ricciardi. The group membership problem in asynchronous systems, Ph.D. thesis, Cornell University, 1992.

[133] Ripple. Ripple homepage. https://ripple.com/

[134] M. Rosenfeld. Analysis of hashrate-based double spending. http://arxiv.org/abs/1402.2009, 2014.

[135] A. Sapirshtein, Y. Sompolinsky, and A. Zohar. Optimal selfish mining strategies in bitcoin. http://arxiv.org/pdf/1507.06183.pdf, 2015.

[136] F. B. Schneider. Implementing fault-tolerant services using the state machine approach: A tutorial. Volume 22, pages 299–319. ACM, 1990. DOI: 10.1145/98163.98167.

[137] O. Schrijvers, J. Bonneau, D. Boneh, and T. Roughgarden. Incentive compatibility of bitcoin mining pool reward functions. In *Proc. of the 20th International Conference on Financial Cryptography (FC'16)*, 2016.

[138] A. Shamir. How to share a secret. Volume 22, pages 612–613. ACM, 1979. DOI: 10.1145/359168.359176.

[139] Y. Sompolinsky and A. Zohar. Accelerating bitcoin's transaction processing. Fast money grows on trees, not chains. *IACR Cryptology ePrint Archive*, page 881, 2013.

[140] Y. Sompolinsky and A. Zohar. Secure high-rate transaction processing in bitcoin. In *Financial Cryptography and Data Security*, pages 507–527. Springer, 2015. DOI: 10.1007/978-3-662-47854-7_32.

[141] Y. Sompolinsky and A. Zohar. Bitcoin's security model revisited. http://arxiv.org/pdf/1605.09193, 2016.

[142] D. Stebila, L. Kuppusamy, J. Rangasamy, C. Boyd, and J. G. Nieto. Stronger difficulty notions for client puzzles and denial-of-service-resistant protocols. In *Cryptographers Track at the RSA Conference*, pages 284–301. Springer, 2011. DOI: 10.1007/978-3-642-19074-2_19.

[143] T. Swanson. Consensus-as-a-service: A brief report on the emergence of permissioned, distributed ledger systems. http://www.ofnumbers.com/wp-content/uploads/2015/04/Permissioned-distributed-ledgers.pdf, 2015.

[144] N. Szabo. Shelling out: The origins of money. http://nakamotoinstitute.org/shel ling-out/, 2002. Accessed: 2017-06-09.

[145] S. Toueg. Randomized asynchronous byzantine agreements. In *Proc. of the 3rd Annual Symposium on Principles of Distributed Computing*, pages 163–178. ACM, 1984. DOI: 10.1145/800222.806744.

[146] P. Veríssimo. Uncertainty and predictability: Can they be reconciled? In *Future Directions in Distributed Computing*, pages 108–113. Springer, 2003. DOI: 10.1007/3-540-37795-6_20.

[147] M. Vukolić. The quest for scalable blockchain fabric: Proof-of-work vs. BFT replication. In *International Workshop on Open Problems in Network Security*, pages 112–125. Springer, 2015. DOI: 10.1007/978-3-319-39028-4_9.

[148] M. Vukolić. Eventually returning to strong consistency. https://pdfs.semanticsch olar.org/a6a1/b70305b27c556aac779fb65429db9c2e1ef2.pdf, 2016.

Authors' Biographies

ALJOSHA JUDMAYER

Aljosha Judmayer received a master's degree in Software Engineering and Internet Computing at the TU Wien. He has five plus years experience in penetration testing as an IT security consultant. At the moment, he is working as an IT security researcher at SBA Research, where he is also working toward his Ph.D. degree on applications of cryptographic currencies and resilience aspects of distributed systems. His research interests include cryptographic currency technologies as well as network and systems security.

NICHOLAS STIFTER

Nicholas Stifter received a master's degree in Computer Science Management and a bachelor's degree in Software Engineering from Vienna University of Technology. He is currently working toward a Ph.D. on security and maintainability aspects of blockchain technologies and smart contracts, and his research interests include Nakamoto consensus, distributed agreement protocols, and computing education for distributed systems topics.

KATHARINA KROMBHOLZ

Katharina Krombholz is a post-doctoral security researcher at SBA Research in Vienna, Austria, and a university lecturer for digital forensics at the Vienna University of Technology and the FH Campus Vienna University of Applied Sciences. She completed her Ph.D. in 2016 with distinction. Her research focuses on usable security, privacy, and digital forensics.

EDGAR WEIPPL

Edgar Weippl is Research Director of SBA Research and associate professor at TU Wien. After graduating with a Ph.D. from the TU Wien, Edgar worked in a research startup for two years. He then spent one year teaching as an Assistant Professor at Beloit College, WI. From 2002 to 2004, while with the software vendor ISIS Papyrus, he worked as a consultant in New York, NY, and Albany, NY, and in Frankfurt, Germany. In 2004 he joined the TU Wien and founded the research center SBA Research together with A Min Tjoa and Markus Klemen. Edgar is a member of the editorial board of *Computers & Security* (COSE), organizes the ARES conference, and is General Chair of SACMAT 2015, PC Chair of Esorics 2015, and General Chair of ACM CCS 2016.

Printed in the United States
by Baker & Taylor Publisher Services